NOT RIGHT IN THE HEAD

MICHELLE WYATT

ALLEN&UNWIN
SYDNEY · MELBOURNE · AUCKLAND · LONDON

The SAGE Test, beginning on page 228, is reproduced with the express permission of The Ohio State University.

First published in 2016

Copyright © Michelle Wyatt 2016

Allen & Unwin
83 Alexander Street
Crows Nest NSW 2065
Australia
Phone:(61 2) 8425 0100
Email: info@allenandunwin.com
Web: www.allenandunwin.com

Cataloguing-in-Publication details are available
from the National Library of Australia
www.trove.nla.gov.au

ISBN 978 1 76029 056 6

Set in 12.5/19 pt Chapparal Pro by Bookhouse, Sydney
Printed and bound in Australia by Griffin Press

10 9 8 7 6 5 4 3 2 1

To my dad, whose unwavering love and dedication should be bottled and handed out to couples around the world

Contents

1

Mrs Pitt's gone shopping

One of my earliest childhood memories is lying in bed at night and hearing my mother yell into the phone, 'Mum—don't forget to hang up the phone!' More yelling, and then eventually the sound of my mother placing the receiver down, followed by a deep grumbling that only pure frustration can conjure. Shortly afterwards, Dad would enter the bedroom I shared with my sister, scoop us out of bed and bundle us into the car for a late-night drive to the Melbourne suburb of Collingwood. We would lie in the back of the family wagon (and when I say lie, I literally mean lie; no seatbelts were required back then, so my sister and I would lie top-to-tail across the back seat)—and, after a fifteen-minute drive, Dad would announce our arrival into the 'spotting zone'. We weren't going to my nan's house to deal with phone-gate. Nan didn't have a telephone so would use various public phone booths around her neighbourhood to keep in touch. Which one she used on any particular day or night was anyone's guess. My sister and I would try to keep our overtired eyelids open enough to locate the one dimly lit phone booth with the swinging handset somewhere within Nana's neighbourhood, motivated by the prize of a Caramello Koala chocolate for the first one to spot it.

Back in those days, if someone phoned you landline to landline and didn't hang up at their end, your phone was rendered useless until their receiver was placed properly back in its cradle—otherwise the call was still effectively active. We would often hear Mum pick up the phone, only to start yelling into the receiver the name of the person she last spoke to. Usually it was Nana.

It wasn't as if Nana meant to cause such an upheaval every time she rang late at night—in fact, Nana probably didn't even remember she had called at all by the time she walked back through her front door.

Nana had Alzheimer's.

The phone calls didn't always end in a late-night family expedition to locate and replace the dangling handset. Sometimes Nana would call to say the power in her house had gone out and none of her lights were working. These calls usually resulted in Dad flying solo; the phone-booth journey required a driver and a spotter, hence the family excursion. It was always a case of Nana having not turned the lights on, and I found it so peculiar that she didn't know how to turn the lights on and off on her own.

Then we'd get calls from her neighbours and friends informing us of Nana's latest adventures. The lady who lived next door would call and simply say, 'Mrs Pitt's gone shopping.' Sounds innocent enough, except those calls would always come between the hours of 1 a.m. and 4 a.m. I still have visions of Nana tottering into town in her dressing gown—buttoned unevenly, of course—handbag clenched firmly under her arm, stopping only to check, every block or so, under the guidance of a flickering street lamp, that she had the house keys.

In the early days, Nana would catch the tram to our house every Saturday morning and spend the day; if Mum and Dad were heading out to the local dinner dance later that evening, she would stay the night and look after us kids. I must have been about six or seven when I noticed she was 'acting weird'. My sister was four years older than me, and my brother, being ten years older, was probably not around as much. He had little tolerance for Nana's shortcomings: she was a big part of our lives, and my brother had obviously witnessed firsthand the decline in her mental state—but all I ever knew was a nana who was a bit different. Much of the time spent at our house would involve her wandering around asking if anyone had seen her keys. They were always in her bag—just where they were last time she checked. My brother was so annoyed one afternoon that he got some ribbon, threaded her keys onto it and hung it around her neck! I guess the frustration of such adverse behaviour in our loved ones can drive us to the edge. I remember it used to make me laugh. To me, as an innocent kid, Nana was hilarious.

Forty years ago, many older people, rather than being diagnosed as having Alzheimer's or dementia, were simply considered 'senile'. And to be fair, the older generation were living in a swiftly changing world, in which technology was progressing at a rapid rate. Even small changes such as circular dials on phones changing to push buttons were advances people like my nana had to get their already muddled heads around. The decimal system had also changed from pounds and shillings to dollars and cents, so paying the conductor for her tram ride required a little extra mental power. When your brain is also starting to decline, life can become very confusing!

Nana had to manually light her gas fireplace with a match, and the carpet in front of it had several burn marks where she would just drop the lit match. She started leaving the gas stove on, so my cousin would call in on her way home from work each night and take the knobs off the stove, just in case Nana decided to whip up a little midnight snack and leave the gas running; my uncle would stop by each morning on his way to work and put the knobs back on. As her dementia worsened, Nana would spend all day wandering around the city and arrive back home around 5 p.m. A little sit down on the couch to rest would result in a two-hour nap. During daylight saving, it was still light when she woke around 7 p.m., so Nana would think she had slept all night and totter off into town for the day, only to find it all dark and deserted by the time she got there. More confusion.

My mum, unlike her sister, had a driver's licence, so she was the one called upon when anything went wrong with Nana. When all of this was going on, Mum was about the same age as I am now. I have no idea how she coped with the constant worry and disruptions—trying to look after three kids, with my dad often away through the week working.

It should have been enough to drive her crazy.

Maybe that's exactly what it did.

•

Alzheimer's is a tough topic to write about with any kind of light-heartedness, so I have tried to get the balance right. This is not a self-help book, nor is it a medical guide, unless my Dr Google skills are valid enough to earn me the letters MD at the end of my name. Instead, throughout this book, I share stories of my own family's experiences, and also the stories of others who have lived through this disease. I also try to offer a general understanding of the disease, its possible symptoms, and how it progresses. My lawyers probably want me to say something here like, 'This book does not endorse any therapy or drug use in the prevention or treatment of Alzheimer's'— and I agree, I endorse nothing (unless I am offered copious amounts of money to do so and even then the lawyers would put the kybosh on it). At the end of the book you'll find a list of helpful Alzheimer's organisations and websites, if you feel the need for more information and support.

I guess the main catalyst for writing this book was a desire to share my family's personal story, but also to reassure people who are caring for a loved one with Alzheimer's that they are not alone, and that others are going through very similar scenarios. I still grieve daily for the loss of my beautiful mother, and I see my father's constant struggle to continue on without her. But as a family we got through it—and what ultimately did get us through was allowing ourselves to smile and laugh occasionally at some of the unusual and challenging circumstances that arise when caring for someone with Alzheimer's.

I'm not suggesting for a moment that, for anyone who has a loved one living with Alzheimer's or dementia, life is a walk in the park and a reason for laughter—even to this day I find it heartbreaking to see what this disease does to people. I don't laugh at the disease or anyone who has it, but when you are confronted with something so challenging that pushes your comfort levels, it's important to find something to help you deal with it—and to quote a cliché, sometimes laughter can be the best medicine.

We found as a family that sharing these stories and finding the occasional moment to see the funny side helped us cope— and still does to this very day.

It's comforting, even if just for a minute.

2

Leaving on a jet plane

I was the youngest of three children and, being the last to flee the nest, had a special relationship-cum-friendship with my parents. Even though I had been reminded way too often that I was an 'accident'—they wanted just a boy and a girl, and then they got me as well—I think this in some way made me closer to Mum and Dad. My brother used every opportunity to remind me of my accidental status, and often when we were fighting he would tell me that I was actually adopted; I never believed him, knowing I was just a victim of the 'third child syndrome'. During regular slide nights with the extended family, he would also take great delight in pointing out the dearth of photos of me as a baby—and the photos I did appear in often captured just the top of my head, with my brother and sister sitting or standing either side. Framing and composition were not my parents' strong suit. Luckily that phase of my brother's teasing only lasted a couple of years. When it became evident that my sister was the smart one of the family, his attention turned towards her and she has copped it ever since.

It seemed like it was often just me and my folks hanging out as I coasted through my teenage years. This closeness continued well into my adult life and I counted my parents as two of my best friends. Dinners out with my friends were often attended by my folks, and their house was open all hours. They were the kind of parents who allowed us to follow our dreams with just the right amount of sensible guidance and support. I knew from an early age that I wanted to work in the television industry, so they totally supported my passion and Mum would chauffeur me to and from job interviews from the age of sixteen. Whatever happened in our personal or work life, they would always have our backs, and there would always be a bed at the house for us and our friends.

I was one of those kids who hated sleepovers and school camp. I barely spent a night away from my parents, and even when I left home at eighteen, I called them every day and visited at least twice a week—mainly for the home-cooked meals and laundry services. Even once I was holding down a well-paying job, Dad would always walk me out to the car and hand me twenty dollars for petrol money.

Just before my twenty-eighth birthday, an opportunity arose to move to the United States for a job. I couldn't pass up the chance, but the idea of living overseas was rather daunting, not just for me, but my parents as well.

Once I'd made the decision to go, it seemed like I couldn't go to any supermarket or shopping mall without hearing 'Leaving on a Jet Plane' streaming over the speakers. That song had always made me cry, even from a young age. To be honest, every John Denver song has that effect on me, but this one in particular could take me from zero to 'it's just the pollen in the air' in seconds.

My parents were excited and heartbroken as they waved me off at the airport terminal with tears in their eyes. Mum insisted that I give her a signal, once I was on the plane, to let her know everything was okay. I'm not sure what she'd imagined could go wrong during the journey from the departure lounge to the actual plane—those loading ramps can be very tricky. Back then, you could actually go out to a viewing deck and watch the planes take off, so I knew Mum and Dad would be out there in the freezing cold, waiting for my signal. I leant across the other passengers seated in my row and asked if they could raise and lower the window shutter a few times. If nothing else, I'm sure this request signalled to my seat buddies that, for the next thirteen hours, the 'crazy woman in 26C' was probably someone they didn't really want to chit-chat with.

So I had fled the nest—but I still rang my parents every day to share my daily experiences, which they lapped up. During these phone calls I could always tell when Mum had visitors in the house. She would know it was me as soon as she picked up the receiver and heard the international dial tone. A pause at her end to make sure her guests were listening, and then she'd say, 'Hello, darling, are you calling all the way from America?' It was her way of bragging to her friends that her daughter was living overseas. How terribly exotic it must have been for those ladies sitting at Mum's kitchen table, sipping their cups of tea and nibbling on nutloaf. I would always cut these conversations short—it got a little tiresome to hear her repeat every detail of our phone call to her eager audience.

'Oh, you took a subway to Central Park . . . You wandered down Fifth Avenue . . . You ate a bagel for breakfast . . .'

I flew them out to visit me a number of times in the US, the first time to stay with me in New York City. Prior to that, the furthest they'd ever travelled was to Tasmania, so that trip was a big adventure for 'Ma and Pa white-bread working-class Australia'. I pushed their boundaries with as many cultural challenges as I could and they loved it. They even managed to head off on a five-day rail adventure along the east coast of the United States, ending up in Boston. I was so proud of how brave and self-sufficient they were, as I thought such adventures would be way beyond their comfort zone. Thinking back, I did notice that Dad was doing a lot of the planning and directing, but I just assumed he was trying to let Mum enjoy the trip without the pressure of organising everything. (Many years later I learnt that on that first trip over, they'd arrived at the departure terminal of Melbourne airport without their passports. Mum was sure she had them, but when she opened her handbag at the check-in counter—ba-bung!—no passports. Luckily my parents had reached the age where they turned up at least two hours early for everything, so my sister called a family friend and navigated them to the hidden spare key at our house so they could drive the passports to the airport— probably with still enough time for my parents to be first in line for boarding.)

Each time they made the trip overseas to visit, I would notice they had both slowed down just that little bit. They were getting old and I wasn't seeing them every day, so those little changes that go unnoticed seeing someone face to face every day become big changes when six months to a year have passed without seeing them. I spent almost ten years living overseas, and returned home to find a very different mother to the one I'd left. I had no idea her 'memory' was getting so bad.

It's funny how you can spend your life expecting something to happen, and then when it does, you don't even realise it's upon you. Nana had Alzheimer's and we all joked that Mum would also end up with it. Even Mum would often say, 'If I end up like Nana, please just put me in a home.' (When I was about ten Nana took me aside and whispered to me, 'Whatever you do, don't let them put me in a home.' That memory always appears in my head like something out of a Harry Potter movie. Not sure what I could have done at the tender age of ten to stop that happening, but I did feel resentment towards my mother and my aunt when they eventually did put Nana in a home.)

So we'd make fun of Mum every time she forgot a name, or called us by the wrong name. Oh yes, we were hilarious. We then started to notice that she wasn't joining in the conversation much, and was just adding the odd 'yes' and 'that's right' here and there. I would call to chat on the phone and ask what she'd been doing: 'Oh, bits and pieces.' Bits and pieces was all I could get out of her, until she'd eventually say, 'I'll just get your father.' Still, we put this down to nothing more sinister than Mum getting a bit doddery and forgetful.

The other thing about Mum is that she was a bit of a hypochondriac. Once I'd moved out of home, I would call her if I wasn't feeling well, and no matter what ailment I had, Mum also had it—and that included one instance where I twisted my ankle doing tae-kwon-do; she too had a bit of a dodgy ankle that day. Having a hypochondriac in your life does weird things to your ability to sympathise when they might actually be sick. Mum was usually healthy, but on the days when she was off colour, or not quite herself, I tended to let it pass over me, assuming she was perhaps dramatising the situation. I probably wasn't as proactive as I should have been, and I carry that baggage with me to this day. To be honest, I still have that lack of empathy for sickness. If my husband is down and out with the flu, my care strategy is to suggest he take a brisk walk around the block to shake it off. My own son at the age of two and a half broke his wrist in two places, and for three days I told him to 'Toughen up, Tiger' with a ruffle of the hair. (In my defence, we didn't realise he'd actually broken his wrist, as he could move and twist his wrist with no pain—but obviously I didn't go on to win Mother of the Year.)

So Mum was gifted with sympathetic illness, shall we say—but she also had another affliction worthy of an entry in *Ripley's Believe It or Not!* Mum could eat a meal and within five minutes, it would have passed through her system and made its way out of her colon. We would sit down for a family dinner and no more than two minutes after finishing, Mum would excuse herself, then arrive back at the table three minutes later claiming she'd 'lost the lot'. That was just gross on many levels, but would also infuriate my brother no end. He would forever be arguing that she did not in fact have a pipe that ran directly from her mouth to her bum that would result in food passing through her system in under five minutes.

'Well I do,' Mum would state proudly.

I looked forward to going to restaurants, where Mum would finish a beautiful meal, visit the restroom, rejoin the table and announce: 'Well, *that* was an absolute waste of money!' Maybe that's how she kept her slender figure all those years. She also had a freakish ability to overhear conversations. In restaurants we'd be continually 'shooshed' so she could get the exact details of all the financial problems the couple three tables away were experiencing. But her powers extended far further than that: she could even hear conversations that were taking place at least two suburbs away. Coming home from school I would be whispering an elaborate plan to my sister of how I was going to dodge my homework that night, and Mum would be standing at the front gate saying, 'I heard that.' She earnt the name 'antenna ears' from all three of her loving children.

Her body was indeed a marvel of science.

Once Dad retired he was home all the time and started doing everything for her. He didn't like her driving at night, and then didn't like her driving at all. He would do the shopping, often cook their dinner—and eventually started finishing sentences for her. I'd get frustrated by this, and chastise him about letting Mum do things for herself. I was so convinced her brain was slowly shutting down that I'd buy puzzles and games for her as stimulation, only to find them tucked away in the sewing cupboard, along with stacks of other unused brain busters, reams of fabric and unpainted china. As a child, Mum was quite the Liberace (in a less bejewelled, flamboyant way), so I set up a digital piano on the back patio, hoping that might help awaken her brain. I also hooked up a computer in the spare bedroom, thinking they could spend lovely afternoons on the 'world wide web' looking at gardening websites and checking in with family via email and poking their friends on Facebook. Granted, the computer was a big ask, as neither of my parents had ever used one, and when I tried to get Dad to type his name it immediately became evident that his fingers had never even graced a keyboard.

As much as I wanted to gracefully bring my parents into the twenty-first century, there are some things that are not worth the effort. (Even today he struggles with his mobile phone, and I can't remember how many times we made the trip to the house because the cable television 'wasn't working'.) Ironically, Mum had a better handle on technology than Dad before she went downhill—but fifteen minutes into our first computer session, I walked back in to find her sliding the mouse across the computer screen. Maybe she was ahead of her time and was 'swiping'. Maybe not. The computer was turned off and never used again.

There is currently no cure for Alzheimer's or dementia. But the big question that everybody continues to ask is: can we do anything to help lessen our chances of getting this disease?

The research is still very inconclusive. Many studies are showing that although you can't repair damaged brain cells, learning something new can create new connections between brain cells, which can in turn increase 'brain reserve'. And if brain cells are damaged by a disease such as Alzheimer's, having a high reserve of healthy brain cells may help the brain to function using different cognitive pathways and strategies, or may help delay the onset of Alzheimer's symptoms.

There is some research to suggest that living a brain healthy life, particularly during mid-life, may reduce a person's risk of developing dementia. Cognitively stimulating activities such as learning a new language or musical instrument, or just listening to radio or reading, can help protect against neural decline.

I had seen all the news stories that get wheeled out every few months claiming that keeping your brain active can help you avoid Alzheimer's. I had seen the junk adverts on websites about brain-training programs that will help keep your mind healthy. Computerised brain training is a billion-dollar industry these days: I just typed 'brain training' into Google and got almost 30 million results. I then typed 'brain training games' and came up with 22 million results, and 14 million results for 'brain training apps'.

I am guilty of buying into the brain training phenomena. When I first decided to get on board, I downloaded every version of every app I could find. I have spent so many hours lying in bed at night swiping arrows, tapping on coloured dots, trying to remember patterns and tapping 'yes' when I should have tapped 'no' that there's a good chance I have lost healthy brain cells through stress and lack of sleep.

There is no evidence to prove that any of these cognitive games or apps are effective in the ways that most of us are shelling out the cash for. They all promise to improve our memory, attention and problem solving, but in reality, at best, they may only improve or extend our ability to perform particular tasks better.

One article I read sums it up beautifully. If the time and money you invest on brain games is time not spent exercising, or learning a language, or trying out a new recipe or playing with your children or grandchildren, then it may not be worth it. But, if you are playing brain games instead of sitting in a sedentary state watching mindless televisions shows, or playing gaming machines for money, then brain training might just be the better choice.

Still, I'm not seeing any quick fixes here.

3

'Twas the Night Before Alzheimer's

The decline that occurs with Alzheimer's can be so slow as to be barely perceptible; many people just accept that as you get older you start to lose your memory, and that's what we assumed was happening to Mum—until the Christmas of 2005, when things started unravelling.

It was a week or so before Christmas Day, and something Mum said hit me like a ton of bricks. Something so out of character I felt my stomach drop, as if I'd just plummeted off the edge of a cliff.

Every year for as long as I could remember, Mum would bake Christmas cookies for friends and family. Intricate little creations that were so perfectly executed and so beautifully decorated it was almost a shame to eat them. I had told Mum that I'd come over and help her start the Christmas cookie process—spending the day in the kitchen with Mum was seeing her at her happiest; she was the ultimate baker, and the pantry was always jam-packed with her delicious cookies, slices and cakes. (Afternoon tea, by the way, was a ritual in our house. Dad was the tea aficionado: one spoon of tea leaves per person and one for the pot, add the boiling water and leave the pot to sit for ten minutes, then three turns to the left and three turns to the right. He used the same teapot for over twenty years and never once washed it out; instead he would empty the tea leaves in the backyard, under the apricot tree. You couldn't have a cup of tea without something to nibble on, so out would come Mum's Anzac bikkies or lemon cake or yo-yos. To this day I blame Mum for my sweet tooth—that and the Caramello Koala phone-booth-spotting game.)

So, the Christmas cookie session was underway. We had all the ingredients lined up—flour and sugar meticulously measured, trays lined, everything working like a well-oiled machine. As Mum began kneading her shortbread dough, she started getting frustrated that it wasn't coming together as it should. I was startled by her potty-mouthed reaction to the disaster unfolding before our very eyes.

As a good-mannered, god-fearing mother of three, Mum was never much of a swearer. In fact she and her sister had a habit of spelling out words that were not fit for little human ears. A lunch session around the kitchen table with the two of them in full flight was like an episode of *Wheel of Fortune*—but without the annoying spinning wheel sound. 'I said to them all, you're giving me the S–H–I–T–S!' or 'She can be a real B–I–T–C–H' or 'He was a proper B–A–S, that one!' The more colourful the swear word, the fewer letters they would use.

So back to the shortbread, which was a crumbled mess. When I suggested that perhaps we could try adding a little more water to soften up the dough, she looked around and said, 'We don't have any more water.' Ummm, yes we do: we are in the kitchen, standing next to a sink equipped with two taps in perfect working order—of course we have water. We can just turn around, turn on the tap and voilà, we have water.

That was the moment I realised that the inevitable was actually happening. That one comment took me from 'Mum is a bit forgetful in her old age' to *'Mum has lost her mind!'* I then began going over all those odd behaviours that had probably been obvious signs of Mum's impending Alzheimer's, but that I hadn't wanted to recognise or acknowledge. The evidence was presenting itself every day: the horse had bolted.

Christmas was always Mum's favourite time of year. She'd spend 364 days planning for it. The kind of planning that saw her hit the shops on Boxing Day to buy discounted wrapping paper and cards for the following year. She would put so much thought and effort into every gift, so all her children had exactly the same number of presents on Christmas morning. Walking into our lounge room after Santa had been was like walking into a room where a Toys R Us truck had been sick all over the floor. Even at an age when we actually knew better, we still bought into the Santa routine as it clearly made Mum happy. You couldn't move for gifts—and we were by no means a rich family, it was just that every little thing was individually wrapped: each pair of undies, each item of doll's clothing that she had hand sewn, every single piece of cheap costume jewellery (that would be broken by the time we sat down for Christmas dinner). And then there were the gifts that kept appearing every year as part of the Christmas ritual. My brother still to this day can't face Christmas without one of those chocolate bar–filled Santa stockings (which are now half the size, ten times the price and packed in plastic rather than netting). Mine was a new purse, always with a coin in it, as it was bad luck to gift a purse without money inside.

After all the presents had been opened, the roast would go in the oven and the smell would permeate the house for the rest of the day. Mum would always fill two crystal dishes to the brim with mixed nuts and chocolate-coated almonds for our pre-dinner nibbles. The table would be set with the good cutlery and special Wedgwood dinner plates; cranberry sauce, apple sauce and gravy all had their own little jugs just for the occasion. The Christmas crackers on the side plates had to be pulled early into the meal, so we could sit around the table in our finest attire and accessorise our outfits by wearing brightly coloured cheap paper crowns on our heads. Christmas carols would croon from the stereo and the calico-wrapped plum pudding, filled with threepence, would be cut down from the bathroom shower rail, where it had been hanging for the past month. (We actually couldn't shower for a month before

Christmas because we didn't want to get the plum pudding wet. Luckily we had a bathtub, otherwise it would have been a very whiffy December.)

Every Christmas Day planned to perfection—it is such a strong memory for me. No matter what was going on in the world or in our individual lives, Christmas dinner at Mum and Dad's was always the same: perfect!

So that first Christmas when things weren't as they'd always been was the real eye opener for us. The tree just didn't look right; normally it would be adorned with family heirloom decorations that each had their own backstory, way too much tinsel and enough flashing lights to cause a seizure—but not this year. A box or two of unused decorations still sat in the spare room, untouched. There were hardly any presents under the tree, and it was horrifyingly obvious there'd be no overpriced, undersized, chocolate-filled plastic Santa stocking for my 50-year-old brother that year. The present-opening ceremony was over in the blink of an eye. I had scored a diary and a few cooking utensils; I looked down at my pile and selfishly felt a little underwhelmed. The only consolation was looking around at everyone else's underwhelming piles. On the upside, it was the first year I didn't have to open the gift of a homemade T-shirt and hold it up saying how beautiful it was.

Then I noticed there was no Christmas card for Dad under the tree. Mum and Dad were huge on writing cards for each other—they would forgo presents for the sake of a beautifully worded card. Mum kept every card she had ever received from Dad and us kids over the years. When I asked her discreetly where Dad's card was, she looked at me blankly. I took her out into the kitchen to find the card, assuming she *had* actually bought one for him—thankfully it was sitting on the bench behind a bunch of unopened mail. As it turns out, Dad probably bought his own card for Mum to give to him. I told her to write on it while I went back into the lounge room to cover up the stealth last-minute card-writing operation occurring in the kitchen. When I went to check on her, she was standing at the bench looking out the window—the card was still blank. She looked at me, tears rolling down her cheeks. She knew something was wrong. She couldn't articulate on the card what was in her head. She couldn't write on her own husband's Christmas card, and that was a truly horrible moment for her. I wanted to hug her, but part of me felt that if I acknowledged this was a thing, I couldn't then deny it was happening. I wrote on it for her, and although Dad knew it wasn't Mum's writing (I tried to fudge it as best I could) he proudly read it aloud after it miraculously turned up under the plastic tree.

That was a bombshell for me, not only in terms of my Mum's future, but for our future as a family—I knew we were all going to have to step up. Mum was no longer capable of being the present buyer, or the tree decorator, or the plum pudding maker, or the buyer of that obligatory chocolate stocking—it was now up to the rest of us to share the load that she had carried for the past 50 years.

I can't say that Mum ever really knew she had Alzheimer's—
we didn't sit her down after her diagnosis and give her the
news, and I'm not sure she really processed what the doctor
had said; we just let her continue her day-to-day life, doing
what we could to keep up appearances. But that Christmas
morning was the only time I could tell she was aware enough
to know something wasn't right. I never saw it in her again.
There is no way Dad couldn't have noticed her downward
spiral, and in hindsight it was obvious that he too covered
up as many of Mum's slip-ups as he could.

There was one particular slip up I wished he'd intercepted.

When I was living overseas, Mum was always so organised and thoughtful in sending gifts over for me to open on
Christmas Day. My last Christmas in the States I spent with
my then-boyfriend, now-husband, and was so excited to open
the box that Mum had sent me, wrapped in Aussie-themed
Christmas paper. I was imagining all the possible gifts that
might be hiding inside. Would there be a new pair of UGG
boots maybe, and a few packets of Tim Tams and Twisties?

Nope. The box, mainly filled with screwed-up newspaper,
contained a travel roulette game, and a skimpy pair of black
lace G-string undies. I'm not sure who was more shocked, him
or me. He must have felt he was about to marry a woman
whose mother thought she was a pole-dancing gambler. That
perhaps should have been a bit of a red flag—not for my
husband, in his choice of a future wife, but for me, about
Mum's state of mind.

That 'not quite right' Christmas, together with Mum's increasing vagueness and the decline in her conversation, prompted us to seek a professional opinion from an Alzheimer's specialist. Mum, Dad and us three kids all sat in the clinic while they conducted a series of cognitive tests. One of them was a verbal questionnaire about general knowledge and current events: what's your name, where do you live, what year is it, who is the prime minister? (Mum could've been forgiven for getting that last question wrong, given the rate Australia changes prime ministers!) She did pretty well on that test—probably a bit better than I would've, if I'm being completely honest. Then she took some logic tests, with questions like draw the hands on the clock to indicate midnight, or what do these animals have in common; with these she struggled. The other tests were of a medical nature.

I walked out of the specialist's office quite uneasy. It was becoming all too real.

A week or two later, we were all back in that same office. When the doctor confirmed that Mum was indeed presenting with the initial symptoms of probable Alzheimer's disease, I didn't believe him.

All this evidence—physical and neurological examinations, psychiatric assessment, MRIs, blood and urine tests, her family history of the disease, and her obvious behavioural changes—and I was still telling myself that if we got her brain active again, she'd be as right as rain.

So what does one do after a diagnosis like that? It would be unlikely we would see any major effect or change in Mum immediately. It's not like we can take any real steps to stop this happening, or start the process of curing or preventing. As a family we didn't really talk much about it. Deep down we all kind of knew it was coming but now it was officially here none of us were really willing to acknowledge it or in fact discuss it. Sure there would be steps that we would need to take down the track, but with Alzheimer's the future is so uncertain. No timelines, no recommended lifestyle or dietary changes—just as you were until you are no more. As much as I was still convinced she was suffering from an over-caring husband, my dad didn't seem to acknowledge the diagnosis at all.

As we left the doctor's rooms I seem to recall my sister and I being a little emotional. It wasn't quite a 'group hug' scenario but we definitely stood around as a family and bonded in the moment. My brother made a comment about how we had just been told something we knew was coming anyway. He had verbalised it but the rest of us weren't there yet.

My sister and brother both went back to work and I took my parents out for a coffee. Just your normal Tuesday morning.

4

Testing the waters

So what is dementia and what is Alzheimer's? Is there a difference? Do people with Alzheimer's always have dementia? Can you have dementia without Alzheimer's? These are questions I am asked on a regular basis. I have to stop wearing that silly T-shirt I bought on my last trip to Bali that says 'Alzheimer's and dementia expert' and a little icon of a thumbs-up under it.

So, what is dementia?

The first thing to note is that dementia is not a disease, it is a condition. In medical parlance, a 'condition' is a broad term that includes all diseases and disorders—so dementia is a collection of symptoms that are caused by diseases or disorders or injuries affecting the brain.

Some of the early symptoms of dementia include memory loss, confusion, changes in personality and behaviour, apathy and withdrawal, and losing the ability to perform everyday tasks.

There are many different forms of dementia, and each has its own causes. The most common types are Alzheimer's disease (which accounts for 50–70 per cent of all dementia cases), vascular dementia, Parkinson's disease, dementia with Lewy body disease, Frontotemporal dementia, Huntington's disease, alcohol-related dementia and Creutzfeldt–Jakob's disease.

Dementia can happen to anybody, but is more common after the age of 65—although it is important to note that dementia is not just a normal part of ageing.

Other medical conditions can also cause symptoms similar to dementia, such as stroke, depression, vitamin deficiencies, hormone disorders, alcoholism, infections, medication side effects or interactions, overmedication and brain tumours.

So, yes, you can have dementia without having Alzheimer's.

What, then, is Alzheimer's?

Alzheimer's disease is named after the German physician, Alois Alzheimer, who first described it in 1906.

Alzheimer's is a disease. It is an irreversible, progressive brain disorder that slowly destroys memory and thinking skills. The disease can be either *sporadic* or *familial*. Sporadic Alzheimer's can affect adults at any age, but usually occurs after the age of 65, and is the most common form. Familial Alzheimer's is a very rare genetic condition caused by a mutation in one of several genes. The presence of these genes means that the person will eventually develop Alzheimer's, usually in their forties or fifties. This form of Alzheimer's disease only affects an extremely small percentage of the Australian population—probably no more than 100 people at any given time.

During the very earliest stage of Alzheimer's disease, people seem to be symptom free; research shows that damage to the brain can actually start a decade or more before memory and other cognitive problems appear. The damage initially appears to take place in the part of the brain that forms memories, and as more neurons die, additional parts of the brain are affected and they begin to shrink.

So, to answer another question. Dementia is actually the *condition*, and Alzheimer's is the *disease* that causes the condition of dementia—which means that if you are diagnosed with Alzheimer's, then you what you actually have is dementia caused by Alzheimer's disease.

I think I've even cleared that up in my own mind now.

Having said this, a diagnosis of Alzheimer's is never really conclusive until a post-death autopsy is performed on the brain—although current advances in brain scanning may soon change this.

Doctors can use a whole range of tests to determine if someone is likely to have Alzheimer's. A complete physical and psychological assessment is undertaken to identify or rule out any other treatable disorders, such as depression or anxiety, that can mimic symptoms of dementia. These tests include blood and urine tests, as well as imaging tests such as X-rays, brain scans and MRIs. There are also cognitive tests to assess the person's memory, problem-solving ability, numerical and counting skills, verbal and written comprehension, and their general ability to carry out activities of daily living.

If you are worried that you or someone you love may have Alzheimer's, the best place to start is your local GP, who can evaluate the symptoms and refer the person onwards for more specialist assessment.

If you are like me and have that nagging voice in the back of your head that kind of wants to know if you're getting Alzheimer's, but doesn't really want to know—but you think it might be handy to have some idea whether you *might maybe* at some point require further testing because you seem to be regularly walking into rooms and forgetting what you walked in there for . . . well, you might be happy to know there are also self-administered tests that you can perform in the comfort of your own home.

One such play-along-at-home test is the Self-Administered Gerocognitive Exam (SAGE), which is included at the back of this book (or you can download it from <http://sagetest. osu.edu/>). It is a brief screening test that can help identify mild cognitive impairment. Actually there are four versions of the SAGE test you can download from that website, but you should choose only one; it doesn't matter which, as they're all interchangeable. The test requires no special equipment, just pen and paper. And no cheating!

I did version four of the test at home. Maybe those brain-training apps have been helping after all, as my score was in the 17–22 points category, which means I am normal, or to be more precise, 'very likely to be normal'.

That sounds more like it.

5

Somebody hide the knives

Mum and Dad had always had the perfect marriage. They met while working together in a department store when Mum was sixteen and Dad was twenty-one. They were married and had their first child, my brother, Peter, by the time Mum was twenty.

They complemented each other perfectly. Dad was the easygoing, never-take-anything-seriously kind of guy, and Mum was the organiser who would always have to pull him into line for goofing around. We spent our childhood laughing at Dad's antics, only to be chastised by Mum; 'Don't encourage him!' she would say.

One of my funniest memories—and also strangest, thinking back on it—was spending many mornings before school searching the house for Mum's false teeth. Having full top and bottom dentures from an early age, Mum would take her teeth out at night and leave them in a glass by the bathroom sink. Dad would wake early for work and, as a morning parting gift to us kids, would hide Mum's dentures somewhere around the house. My poor mum: not only did she spend most mornings trying to get three kids out of bed, clothed, fed and off to school, but she had to do it all while frantically searching high and low for her missing teeth. There were no mobile phones back then, and with Dad on building sites most of the day, she couldn't just call him to uncover their mystery location. So if we couldn't find them, Mum would have to drive us to school toothless, cursing my father the whole time, in a lispy, gummy kind of way. He outdid himself one morning when, after a few laps of the house with no success, I walked into Mum and Dad's bedroom to find her teeth swinging from the ceiling light on a piece of string. Even Mum smiled that day (in a lispy, gummy kind of way).

Aside from the usual shenanigans, our family was a very conventional working-class, white Australian household, except it was matriarchal to its core. What Mum said stood, and Dad would always make sure we didn't do anything to 'upset your mother'. Whenever there were any problems within the extended family, Mum and Dad were the 'go-tos'—the ones everyone sought counsel from. Even to this day, their relationship fills me with wonder and envy.

Dad was very skilful, athletic and handy, but Mum was the creative and artistic one. She always made our clothes—although in hindsight we could have done without that on many occasions. She baked to perfection, and was also very crafty. Once we were all at high school and a little more independent, she joined all sorts of clubs and took all kinds of classes to advance her skills. Eventually she started competing in art shows—cake decorating, floral art, china painting, you name it—and the family house was soon filled with blue ribbons and plaques from her successes.

It seemed so cruel that this disease hit someone who had such an active and creative brain, and who at the age of 65 was still relatively young. But as with so many illnesses, Alzheimer's doesn't discriminate.

A year or two after the initial diagnosis, Mum started to deteriorate into a state we were all dreading. She stopped reading the morning paper, stopped cooking, stopped showing any signs of independence at all. I would frequently get mad at her for not being able to do things—I guess I was still struggling to accept the reality of her disease. Every couple of weeks I would paint her nails, but trying to get her to hold her fingers in the right position was excruciatingly frustrating. There were times I would yank her fingers so hard I was worried I was hurting her—but even that wasn't enough for her to 'snap out of it' and follow what I thought were pretty basic requests, such as 'please keep your hands still'. I'm quite a patient person, but I found myself losing it on more than one occasion. It was a bit like trying to talk to someone who doesn't understand English, when you think that if you talk *s l o w e r* and LOUDER, they will eventually grasp what you are trying to say. How she failed to understand even the most simple instructions was beyond me.

Dad was incredible. He took on the role of carer like a duck to water, taking care of the washing, cooking and other household duties. I still struggle with these routine tasks on a daily basis. At the age of over 70, it was a lot of work for him, both physically and mentally. Luckily my husband and I lived nearby, so we could help him out—but being a traditional Aussie older-generation male, many of our offers of assistance would be met with a 'We'll be right' from Dad.

Caring for Mum became increasingly difficult, however. She became incontinent, and wouldn't eat unless I was there to feed her. We had to install ramps over the steps to ensure she didn't trip, and also had to keep all the doors locked and the knives hidden. I was feeding her dinner one evening and she turned to me, looked into my eyes and said as clear as day: 'I am going to kill you dead with a knife.' I nearly corrected her, saying that if she had killed me with said knife, then I would technically be dead anyway, but went with my better judgement instead and ignored the comment. It was quite ironic, really, as Mum was the most passive, non-confrontational and non-violent person I have ever known.

She would also constantly pace around the house talking to herself. It was fascinating in a way to listen to those conversations. Many of them seemed to be a dialogue between herself and her sister, who had by then died the year before, but I was always a bit worried I might be privy to information that I either didn't want to know, or wasn't meant to know.

We started taking Mum for walks around the neighbourhood—if only to save the carpet she was wearing out around the house. I swear she could have powered a nuclear power station with the energy she exerted walking constantly. It was like watching a baby walk for the first time: we'd stay about three paces behind her in case she veered off in the wrong direction, but she didn't want us to hold her hand or direct where she was going. How odd it must have looked for the neighbours to see Mum walk past—then five seconds later Dad, me, my husband and two dogs in tow, over and over again until it started to get dark, when we would take her inside, in case she fell.

The doctors had Mum on various medications. We all know there is no magic pill that will make this disease go away, or even restore 'normal' functioning. Research has come a long way even since Mum was diagnosed, and we all hope that a cure for Alzheimer's could be just around the corner. Given my family history, I for one am counting on it.

One of the tablets Mum was taking worked to slow down the disease, but over time she became less receptive to its specific effects and would have to be switched to another medication. Mum was also crying a lot of the time, so she was prescribed antidepressants to ease her distress.

We all knew Mum was a bit of a crier, but this was different. These seemed to be tears of sadness and frustration. Who knows what she was feeling and how much she understood or comprehended about her condition. And it wasn't all out sobbing, more just a constant flow of tears which was very distressing to witness. The antidepressants ultimately worked but with that came the dulling of most of her personality. Not exactly a win either way for us, but for her? Who knows.

Besides antidepressants, some other drugs that are commonly prescribed to minimise the agitation and depression that can present in Alzheimer's are antipsychotics, mood stabilisers, anxiety-relieving drugs, cholinergics and anticonvulsant drugs. Some of the side effects of certain medications, or combinations of medications, can outweigh their usefulness, so getting the right balance can be difficult.

Numerous herbal remedies and dietary supplements are also marketed as brain boosters or memory enhancers, but there is little scientific evidence to support their effectiveness. They can also interfere with prescribed medications, so there are legitimate concerns about their use.

Having spent so much time in a dementia ward, it is amazing how Alzheimer's presents differently in everyone. It's a hard task to get the medications just right to make patients comfortable, and at the same time manage their side effects.

Mum didn't experience some of the more challenging side effects—whether that was because her medications suited her, or whether certain personalities just present differently, we really don't know. Some families in the dementia ward had a truly horrible time trying to manage their loved ones, so as frustrating as it was to see Mum in a semiconscious state a lot of the time, we figured that in some ways, it could've been worse.

Some of the more manageable behaviours I have witnessed are anxiety, depression, wandering, fidgeting, shadowing (where a person follows another around at a very close proximity), repetitive behaviour, shouting and screaming, hoarding of other people's belongings and loss of inhibitions. But at the extreme end of the spectrum you will see aggression and violence, both verbal and physical, illusions, hallucinations and psychotic episodes.

6

Everything must go!

We started trying to convince Dad that it would be better for him and Mum to sell the house and move into a retirement village, one that had a nurse onsite and support around the clock. Understandably, Dad hated the idea—his world was unravelling at a rapid rate and he was trying to hold on to what he could. He and Mum had lived in that house for over 50 years—a house in which they had raised three children, five grandchildren and three dogs. You couldn't open a cupboard in the spare room without a memory falling out and hitting you on the head, so Dad was determined that he and Mum would stay in their own home as long as they could.

One morning, Dad rang to say that Mum wasn't right and I should probably come over. When I arrived she was sitting in her usual chair at the kitchen table. The morning newspaper was open in front of her—not that she was capable of actually reading anymore. For as long as I could remember, Mum couldn't function in the morning without toast, tea and a read of the paper, so it was more of a routine thing that Dad was continuing. There were a few pieces of uneaten toast sitting on a plate. When I walked in, she didn't look up at me—instead her head was down and she seemed to be leaning off the chair to the right. Dad said she got up okay that morning, but while she was eating her breakfast, she slowly started to slump over to one side. Her pulse was normal and she didn't feel hot, but to be on the safe side we decided to load her into the car and take her to hospital, to get her checked out.

When we arrived they popped her onto a gurney and positioned us in a cubicle while we waited for a doctor. Mum didn't look like she was in any pain, but seemed a bit more disoriented than usual. When the doctor arrived, he did all the standard tests—blood pressure, temperature and a bit of poking and prodding—but nothing was jumping out at him. He then asked Mum to perform a series of simple tests to rule out stroke. His first request was to raise her right arm. Nothing. The doctor looked at me puzzled.

'She has Alzheimer's,' I offered.

He then asked her to raise her left arm. Again nothing. Another puzzled look.

'She has Alzheimer's,' I repeated, just in case he hadn't heard me.

He then asked Mum to stick out her tongue. This time he didn't even have to look at me as I jumped in rather loudly, 'She *still* has Alzheimer's!'

He turned around and patiently explained it would be hard to get an accurate diagnosis if Mum couldn't perform a basic task. Now clearly my medical expertise doesn't extend much beyond taking a pulse and feeling a forehead, but I did know that Mum wasn't going to respond to any of these requests, as necessary as they were. Of course the doctor needed to rule out other more sinister causes for Mum's turn—but as two of the tell-tale signs for a stroke are disorientation and difficulty speaking or understanding, this could take a while. Given that the doctor seemed to me at the time like he didn't understand my interjections, I had to stop myself from suggesting that maybe he should be conducting these tests on himself. I didn't. Instead I calmly worked with Mum on getting her to stick out her tongue and perform a few simple actions that were required.

Four hours later—or should I say three trips to the vending machine and two cups of horrendous coffee later—we took Mum home with a medical report indicating that she'd most likely suffered a mini-stroke known as a 'transient ischaemic attack', or TIA for short. The signs of a TIA are similar to a stroke, but the effects aren't as long lasting as those of a full-blown stroke.

So Mum was back home, with no obvious signs of being any worse for wear. She was still disoriented, and still had difficulty speaking and understanding—just as she was before the TIA.

This episode, as awful as it must sound, was almost a blessing in disguise, as it jolted Dad into reality. Within a week we were meeting with real estate agents to put the family house on the market. Dad must have wondered what struck him—we were presented with a window of opportunity and we jumped through that window and ran.

Packing up a home that a family has lived in for 50 years is no easy task. Our first decision was whether to sell it as is—a 'renovator's dream'—or to actually renovate it. When you live in a house for as long as my parents had, with no intention of ever leaving, you don't tend to update much. Ours was a humble two-bedroom, one-bathroom weatherboard house on what was a huge block of land for a suburban street. My sister and I had shared a normal-sized bedroom, while my brother had a teeny-tiny room off the kitchen, which Dad built when I 'accidentally' came along. That bedroom was so small that my brother had to leave the room to change his mind, or so Dad used to joke. The house had a large rumpus room at the back, which Dad also built, and which ended up being where most of the socialising took place, as it had big sliding windows that opened into the kitchen—the room Mum spent most of her time in. Whenever we had guests over for dinner, we'd cover the huge snooker table in the rumpus room with a piece of chipboard and a tablecloth to serve as a dining table. Mum didn't like the lounge room getting messy, so that was reserved for after-dinner relaxing and special occasions. A new kitchen was installed in the late 1970s, and the brown laminate cupboards accented with yellow tiles were still in pretty good nick. The lounge had a semi-makeover by way of carpet and a new lounge suite in the 1980s, when Dad won some money on a trifecta. The traffic areas where the shagpile was worn were covered with rugs. There were few modern appliances gracing that house—a colour TV that my parents won in a raffle, and an inbuilt air conditioner they never used. (We would often arrive on a weekend for a summer barbecue and find Mum and Dad sweltering in front of a small oscillating fan. I would remind them they had a perfectly good air conditioner that they could turn on with the touch of a button and be miraculously cool—but no, air conditioners were noisy and used up way too much power.)

In preparation for sale we decided to renovate my brother's broom closet by ripping out all the cupboards and putting a futon/sofa in it, and voilà—a three-bedroom house. The rest of the house we just de-cluttered and freshened up a little. There was talk of pulling down the asbestos garage, but thankfully commonsense (and the law) prevailed and we convinced Dad that it was a much bigger and more involved job than he could possibly pull off by himself. Dad had voiced a desire to just rip out the offending panels, load them into the trailer and take them to the tip, but we decided that when it was time for the garage to meet its maker, it should be done properly—not by a 70-year-old man with a mallet, a pair of overalls and a 50-cent mask from Bunnings over his nose. Yep, let the new owners deal with it. Besides, we weren't covering up the fact that the garage—which I might add was also our playroom/cubby house as kids—had asbestos in the roof. We'd hung out there for the best part of twenty years and we all turned out okay.

De-cluttering a family home basically involves asking all the kids who have long fled the nest to take their old shit away. Yep, that took care of about three cupboards. For years, Mum and Dad had encouraged us to take our old stuff to our own houses. We'd often arrive for a family meal to find Mum had packed a box for us to sort through. We had the option of taking it all home, or she was going to throw it all out—so a trip to Mum and Dad's for dinner usually ended with us leaving with a doggie bag of the past. I would've preferred a doggie bag of roast and trifle, as I had no room in my house for these childhood keepsakes, but it turned out the stuff we didn't take was never actually tossed out, just put straight back into the cupboard, only to greet us again at our next visit. But this time was different, of course, as our family house was going to be sold, which meant there was now a definite deadline for clearing out all our old stuff. We decided upon the most sensible way of dealing with the clutter: a garage sale!

We started sorting though every cupboard, and grouping items into toys, clothes, electronics, kitchen items, etc. I'm a very organised person, so this was right up my alley. I made little signs for each trestle table, and decided every item would be labelled with a price tag. On the day my brother, sister and I would each man a table, and Dad would relay our enormous takings inside the house every twenty minutes. My sister went to the bank to make sure we had plenty of change for our customers, signs went up around the neighbourhood and a notice was printed in the local paper, saying the sale would start at 8 a.m. sharp.

The day arrived and I was there early to set everything up. My sister was running late and my brother texted to say he couldn't make it at all. Right: all going well so far. When my sister arrived at 7.15 a.m. I heard her arguing with a man in the driveway. An eager shopper had arrived early and wanted to be let in; she basically told him to piss off and come back at the advertised time. I was angry that she'd scared away a potential customer, she got upset at me, Mum kept wandering down the driveway in her dressing gown and Dad was taking stuff off the tables that he now decided he didn't want to sell—and the crowds were gathering.

I thought I was prepared for what was about to unfold; I wasn't. Once the gates opened, people started streaming in, and I realised I had clearly underestimated my ability to keep an eye on everything. There were hands going everywhere, customers picking up items and carrying them around, then putting them back down on the wrong table. As a self-confessed control freak, that was doing my head in—but then people were trying to bargain with us while making comments about what our old stuff was actually worth. It was very confronting. How dare somebody say the bike my Dad taught me to ride on wasn't worth $20! It might have been a bit rusty and missing a wheel, but come on, people. Of course that wooden bowl I bought my parents in Bali and snuck through Customs undetected was worth $5—I could've gone to jail for that bowl! It felt like everyone was judging the value of our family memories.

One hour in and the tables were still covered. It seemed like we'd hardly sold a thing—like when you've been eating a big bowl of spaghetti for hours and it looks like you haven't even started. Dad kept coming out every ten minutes to take the cash inside, but would also grab one more keepsake he just couldn't give up—and every time he came out that back door, Mum would follow in her dressing gown and it would take three of us to get her back in the house.

This wasn't running smoothly. We had to take some drastic action, and quickly—so we started writing up '$5 Everything Must Go' signs. I was loading stuff up on that red spot special table faster than I could process what was actually happening.

I'd had some previous experience with this trick, which I'd learnt as a teenager working part time in a department store. A staff member would walk around collecting a trolley full of items from the shelves, priced between $1 and $4. The contents of the trolley would then be transferred to a table set up in the middle aisle of the store. They'd put up an 'Everything $5' sign, plug in a flashing red light—and instant mayhem. Shoppers would flock to snap up a bargain, filling their arms with $5 items that on the shelves were priced at only $2.

Our red spot special table went nuts. Transactions were proceeding at record speed, and my heart couldn't keep up with my brain. I sold my favourite childhood toy for $5. It was a Barbie campervan, the stuff childhood dreams are made of. A luxury vehicle fitted out with every mod con, and enough space to sleep eight cool friends. It had a drop-down ramp at the back, and a vinyl roll-up window on the side—perfect for hanging out at the beach. Barbie had her first kiss in there with Ken. It was the ultimate dream toy—and here I was handing it over to a complete stranger for $5.

At one point my sister came over to say a man was offering $20 for all my old AFL cards. $20? WTF? I'd collected those cards over a number of years. I had every player from every team—it was a complete set with swaps. Those cards would've been responsible for at least two of the fillings in my teeth (each pack of five cards would come with a strip of chewing gum). She sold the lot for $15.

Ultimately, practicality took over. At that time I didn't have a child and, at the age of 41, ever having a child wasn't looking likely. I didn't have that sense of needing to hold on to these keepsakes to pass on to my own children, so what was I going to do with it all, really? It'd only end up sitting in the back of a cupboard or in storage until the day came when someone would be cleaning out all my own cupboards and tossing it all away. I'd spent most of my adult life convincing my parents not to throw out my childhood keepsakes, but when it came time to clean out the family house, I was the first to load it all up on that red spot special trestle table in the driveway.

At the end of the sale, we still had quite a lot of stuff left. Conveniently my brother showed up just as we were packing everything into boxes for charity. He picked through all those items he hadn't seen in two decades but now desperately needed—and the rest went straight into the skip the following weekend.

Eight years on and the mother of a seven-year-old, I still kick myself for what I discarded. My son would have loved those footy cards.

7

Location, location, location

After a few weeks on the market, we received a good offer for the house, and sold before auction. Once again proving that pressure is the ultimate motivator.

The settlement period was 90 days, so the process of finding suitable digs for my parents began in earnest. It quickly became apparent that getting into a desirable retirement village is a bit like getting a child into a prestigious private school: the waiting lists are a mile long! There must be some merit in really planning out your life from the outset. As soon as you consider starting a family, you think about what maternity hospital you want to be in, and once you've had the baby, then begins the process of putting their name down for day care, primary school, secondary school, college and so on—until one day, you are applying for a spot in a retirement village, then a nursing home, and finally, a burial plot. You start out trying to secure your future, and end up looking for somewhere to end it.

So we did the tours of retirement villages. They never really look like the brochures or websites, and shall we just say that the units some of the older ones had available were clearly available for a reason. We needed a place that would help Dad retain his independence, but also cater for Mum's decline. It was also important for them to stay close to their network of friends, so they could visit, and ideally to be within a half-hour drive of at least one of us kids.

It struck me as a little ironic that I lived so close to my parents. When my husband and I moved back to Australia, we looked around for quite a few months before finding a place to live. I remember telling Mum about one particular house we were interested in, but she wasn't impressed with its location. 'Forty-five minutes away is too far for you to be living,' she said, making me instantly feel guilty for having a life. I'd been living in the United States for close to ten years, but all of a sudden, 45 minutes was too far away. We ended up settling on a place only seven minutes from the family home. Her guilt trip had clearly worked.

We chanced upon a new retirement village that was still in the process of being built, and which still had some units available to buy off the plan. The units would be finished just as the 90-day settlement period expired, so the timing was brilliant. It was a little further out than we'd hoped—but upon completion there would be a nursing home onsite, with a fully functioning dementia wing, so it was perfect for Mum and Dad.

For Dad, one of the toughest parts of the move was downsizing. He and Mum were avid gardeners and had amassed over a thousand orchids in the greenhouses in their backyard; Mum would lose a whole day just pottering around in them. They'd both served on various orchid club committees, and much of their later social life was spent with fellow club members, so it was a wonderful hobby for them to be immersed in. However, it quickly became obvious that a thousand orchids were not going to fit in a nine-by-five metre courtyard, so Dad had to give most of his beloved orchids away, which broke his heart a little. Even after we'd set a limit on how many orchids he could take to the new unit, we kept finding extra little pots he'd hidden under other household items during the move.

When we finally got Mum and Dad settled into their lovely new unit, it was a huge weight off our minds, as they were now in a facility that catered for them in all the right ways. It was clean, secure, fitted with all the newest mod cons, and had nurses and caretakers on-call around the clock. It even had an air conditioner that they could refuse to turn on.

I knew this would be a huge lifestyle change for Dad, who by nature was a very independent and stubborn person at the best of times. But even he could see the benefits for Mum so he embraced it. I still don't know whether Mum at that time knew exactly what was happening, but as long as she was with Dad then her world was complete. Within a week they had made friends with all of the residents and we could relax for a while.

We also made an appointment with the nursing home manager to see if we needed to put Mum's name down on a waiting list for full-time nursing home care. But it didn't really work like that, the manager explained, as patients need to be officially admitted to the nursing home based on medical assessment. Meanwhile, we would just have to hope for the best, until that time arose.

So, life was good—or as good as it could be, under the circumstances. Mum and Dad spent most of their days wandering around the village, meeting neighbours for coffee and hanging out in the community centre. We organised a home-care nurse to help with Mum a few days a week, to take the pressure off Dad, so he could spend an hour or two off on his own, doing what he wanted to do. We were starting to worry about his lack of normal interaction with people—the kind where he didn't have to be Mum's interpreter or carer in every social situation. But it turned out that looking after Mum is all Dad really wanted to do, so he would sit and chat with the nurse while she bathed Mum and did some remedial exercise with her.

The Christmas of 2007, the first in the new 'family home', was strange. My sister and I arrived early to prepare the lunch, only to discover that in the downsizing, many of the heavy-duty cooking pots and pans had ended up on the red spot special table at the garage sale. The Christmas tree had no lights on it, someone forgot to buy Christmas crackers, and my brother's chocolate-bar stocking fell through the cracks again. I did, however, have a legitimate excuse for some of my absentmindedness—I'd found out a few weeks prior to Christmas that I was pregnant. I'm pretty sure that 'baby brain' doesn't kick in that quickly—and if I'm telling the truth, I still try to use that excuse to this day. In my mind the 'baby brain' disclaimer has a shelf life of about ten years.

My husband and I were very excited to tell the family of our news. We had been trying to conceive for a long time, and right in the midst of all this parental upheaval, it had finally happened. Mum had always wanted me to have a child, and I had always envisioned telling her being a joyous occasion, but in the end I missed being able to tell her by a few months.

Instead I decided to frame a picture of our ultrasound, wrap it up and give it to Mum and Dad for Christmas.

Dad opened my gift and promptly said, 'What the bloody hell is this?'

Mum was asleep in a chair.

To be fair, when Dad realised the cryptic gift was a picture of his unborn grandson, he was over the moon.

He couldn't stop smiling.

Mum couldn't stop sleeping.

•

About six months after they moved into their new place, I received another one of those 'Your mother's not right' phone calls. This time we called an ambulance, as Mum was getting harder to manage and move around. She had suffered another minor stroke and was admitted to hospital.

We were then faced with deciding whether Mum would be able to go back to their retirement village, or if she now needed to be admitted to a nursing home. That was a bit of a reality shock for all of us.

During her week in hospital, the doctors performed tests to assess Mum's state of health, both physical and mental. We had been through this before: when they asked Mum if it hurt when they poked her, she would say yes. If they'd asked her if she had three heads, she would also have said yes. Why couldn't they figure out she was well beyond the stage of being able to communicate properly?

At 5.45 one morning I got a call from the hospital suggesting I come in as soon as I could, as Mum might be heading towards a cardiac arrest. I made it to her bedside in record time—one of those drives that, on reflection, you can't remember if you stopped for any traffic or red lights. When I arrived, Mum was wired up to a heart monitor; the nurses told me that her heart rate was stable and they were keeping an eye her. I enquired about the events leading up to this new situation; it transpired that when the on-duty nurse checked on her during the early hours and asked Mum if she had pains in her chest, Mum had replied 'Yes'. I suggested that maybe they should have a big sign above the bed with flashing lights that warned 'Unable to answer questions accurately'. If Mum had been in court there would have been an objection about leading the witness. Was I the only one in the room who realised their patient wasn't functioning at full capacity?

The tests finally showed that Mum's overall physical health was stable, but that it would be best for her to go directly from the hospital into full-time nursing home care. I immediately rang the nursing home manager, and as luck would have it, they had a room available. We were so happy. Ironic, isn't it? Being happy that your mother is being admitted into a nursing home—or even more bizarre, a dementia ward?

We were so focused on getting Mum into the nursing home that we went into practical mode, thinking how it would relieve Dad of the burden of taking care of Mum every single minute of every day. It would be the best place for her, and their unit in the retirement village was just a five-minute walk and four-digit passcode away. (A little tip: if you are ever trapped inside a nursing home, and don't know the four-digit passcode, try the postcode.)

We didn't really stop to think what a huge impact it would have on Dad—that he was about to grieve the loss of his life partner. All of a sudden the woman he had woken up with for over 50 years wasn't going to be beside him every day. She had been his whole life, and even more so since she became ill. He had never functioned alone, had never slept alone and had probably never anticipated living alone.

8

Hopelessly devoted

I know there isn't much to laugh about when it comes to Alzheimer's. It is a horrible disease that robs sufferers of their faculties, and more importantly their dignity. It killed me to see my mother, who was once so loving, vibrant, talented and entertaining, sit lifeless in a chair with no idea where she was, or who any of us were. Unable to walk, talk or feed herself. I couldn't help thinking there was no way she would have wanted to continue existing in that state, but therein lies another problem with this disease: there was no way of knowing what was going on in her mind. Did she know where she was and who we were, but just couldn't communicate that to us? The 'nothingness' in her eyes made us believe she had no idea at all, so what was ultimately best for her was hard to know. Watching a parent's decline is devastating. You go back and forth from wanting them to 'hang in there' and fight, to wanting them to be free of the suffering. I'm actually not sure which scenario I was hoping for. Can I say neither?

As hard as it was for us to see Mum like that, it must have been incomprehensible for Dad to deal with, day in and day out. His life changed dramatically when she was admitted to the nursing home, and if we thought he might now gain a little independence and spend just a little time doing something for himself, we were wrong. As the true devoted husband he had been for 52 years, he sat next to my mother, holding her hand, from 8 a.m. until 8.30 p.m., every single day of the year from the day she checked in—or should I say checked out. It goes without saying that we were in awe of his amazing love and care for Mum, but his devotion meant he also missed some important milestones in his children's and grandchildren's lives. A few months after Mum moved into the nursing home, I gave birth to my first and only child—a son. My sister insisted that Dad come to the hospital that night and meet his new grandson; sensing his hesitation, she just turned up at the nursing home and herded him into her car. That night in the hospital was an emotional one for everyone. Dad had very mixed feelings, both of overwhelming joy, but also deep sadness that Mum couldn't enjoy the moment she had looked forward to for so long. Birthday parties, family functions and Easter egg hunts came and went without Dad around. It was very difficult to explain to my son in those early years why

Papa couldn't come along to Grandparents Day at his day care centre or school.

So as well as losing our mother, in a way we felt we had lost our father too. Of course we were infinitely grateful for what he did for Mum—that kind of loyalty and dedication is not found very often. I'd already lost my mother–daughter relationship with Mum years before, and it had taken me a long time to break the habit of reaching for the phone to tell Mum when anything good or bad happened in my life, but once her illness really took hold, Dad was all business and totally preoccupied with her care. He wasn't exactly someone you could whine to when your day was a bit shitty—god knows he had enough on his plate.

Even to this day I'm amazed how quickly Dad adapted to caring for himself. Every night he would cook up a meal of meat and two vegies. He did his own washing, paid his bills and kept the unit in a neat and tidy state. If I fell off the perch tomorrow, within a few days our house would probably look like it had been hit by a bomb and my son would be living on a steady diet of mac and cheese—but Dad had it all sorted, and after spending all day looking after Mum would arrive home with enough will and energy to look after himself.

I rang him every night around 9 p.m. to see how Mum was and how his day had been. By then he would have eaten his dinner and had time to sit down and relax with his second glass of wine. The nightly phone call usually went like this.

'Hi, Dad, how are you?'

'Still here, which is a good start.'

'How was Mum today?'

'She was good. She did everything she had to do, ate her meals, dozed on and off throughout the day, and was sound asleep by the time I left tonight.'

'How was *your* day?'

'Don't get me started . . .' And he'd then give me a blow-by-blow account of every single thing that had gone wrong during the day: Mum's food was cold, they were late taking her to the toilet, they dressed her in the wrong shirt, she was given her tablets fifteen minutes late, they didn't ask if she wanted to go on the bus excursion, the concert in the living area was too loud for her, the woman at her lunch table coughed all the way through the meal . . .

A nursing home is not a hotel. I wish I had a dollar for every time I used that phrase in conversation with my dad during those last few years. If it was a full-service hotel, I would definitely be having a word to the manager, but it wasn't. It was a nursing home, full to the brim with over a hundred low- to high-care patients requiring round-the-clock attention, staffed by fully qualified nurses and carers doing an amazing job. And Mum was one of the lucky ones who had a loved one on hand to keep her company and help with her care. Dad took up the challenge with gusto, and we were very grateful that he did, but I can't begin to imagine how irritating it must've been for the carers to have someone sitting there all day, day in, day out, watching and critiquing their every move. In Dad's eyes, Mum was the most important resident in that facility, and if she wasn't treated like the Queen of England, there'd be trouble. Not only did it take a toll on him, but the carers from time to time would get a little cranky. He didn't seem to pick up on the signs though. Each morning he would arrive before Mum was barely awake and out of bed. If her breakfast wasn't brought in by 8.30 a.m., he was on the warpath. He would stand at the door, wait for the next unlucky carer to walk past and give them a serve. After a while, to avoid an unwarranted earful, the carers would stop walking past Mum's room— which would get him even madder.

We tried to put a 'curfew' on Dad, where he wasn't allowed in the building before a certain hour of the morning, making sure that the directive came from the nursing home and not us—you know, the whole 'good cop, bad cop' theory. It started off at no visits before 10 a.m. We figured this would give him enough time to get up at a leisurely hour, potter around and then meander over to the nursing home. That worked for about a week. It was like we'd enforced a New Year's resolution on him—it was bound to fail. There was nowhere else he wanted to be, and keeping him away just made him more scrutinising of the care she received when he wasn't there: they hadn't given her the right breakfast; she wasn't sitting in the right chair by the right window. God help the staff on the mornings they got sidetracked and she was still tucked up in bed when Dad arrived.

So 10 a.m. became 9.45 a.m., then 9.30 a.m.—and before we knew it, we were right back where we started at 8 a.m.

But it wasn't just the 'service' at the nursing home that got his blood boiling. The residents were also a constant source of frustration. Spending so much time visiting Mum and listening to Dad's stories, we began to care about and empathise with the other patients in the ward, and the lives they too had lost, so I would enquire about certain residents and how they were doing.

The nightly phone conversations would continue.

'Everyone okay in there today?' I'd ask.

'I'm telling you, love, some of them are not right in the bloody head!' he'd grumble.

'No, Dad,' I'd point out, 'they're *not* right in the head—that's why they're in a dementia ward.'

There it is in a nutshell. Each and every patient in the dementia ward wasn't 'right in the head', and none of them were able to function in a 'normal' environment—including Mum, which Dad didn't want to acknowledge. But sad as it all was, I had to admit that some of his stories were highly entertaining. I just needed to sit back and allow myself a moment to smile.

9

The elephant in the room

They say the best thing about Alzheimer's is forgetting you have it. What's the other best thing about having Alzheimer's? Opening your own Christmas presents. Even as I watched my mother slowly deteriorate, I could see the funny side of these jokes.

Maybe because the words *Alzheimer's* and *dementia* have been forefront in my mind for so long, I'm acutely aware of how many times people joke about having the disease whenever they forget what they were saying, or lose track of what they were about to do. 'Must be the Alzheimer's,' they'll quip.

It doesn't bother me when people say that, but those who know my family history almost always feel the need to apologise. I remember having a discussion with a colleague at work a few years ago about his 'great idea' that I had actually suggested to him the day before. When I reminded him that the idea had been on the table the day before, he retorted, 'I think you must have Alzheimer's.' I left the room—not because the comment offended me, but because he was a dick and further discussion would have been fruitless. In his mind, he had touched on a nerve, and he then spent the entire day apologising for his insensitive remark. I let him wallow in his regret—you take what you can get.

Alzheimer's and dementia seem to be the fallback joke for forgetfulness. I'm pretty sure people aren't throwing out 'Must be the cancer' comments on a regular basis. But would anyone who makes such comments in jest—and I'm as guilty as the next guy (if only I could remember his name!)—be so jovial about it if they knew they would indeed fall victim to Alzheimer's or dementia at some point in their life?

Would you want to know?

There are cognitive written tests that can indicate whether you potentially have an underlying problem with your memory—some of which I referred to earlier—as well as tests to determine whether you carry the gene, and your risk of developing the disease. To know or not to know? Either way, it is such a complex dilemma.

On one hand, there is the advantage of foresight in being able to take steps for the future—to put in place a plan for your family and friends in dealing with your decline. But in many cases, this decline can be a very slow and gradual one. Unlike other life-threatening illnesses, Alzheimer's has no 'expected' timeline, apart from certain physical and mental signposts indicating the progression the disease.

My mother assumed she would get Alzheimer's, given that her own mother and sister had succumbed to it at a relatively young age—and she was very adamant that when it *did* happen, we should 'lock her up and throw away the key'. Whenever Mum would say that, we'd joke that we wouldn't need to throw away the key, as she wouldn't be able to remember where we put it. Oh yes, we really were hilarious.

Personally, at this point in time, I don't think I would want to know if I am likely to end up with Alzheimer's. Part of me feels like I'd be buying into a self-fulfilling prophecy. Knowing what lies ahead would probably consume me, and send me down the path quicker than might have normally happened. There is no scientific or logical reasoning behind this thought, but I know how my brain works. I would be self-checking every word I spoke—or didn't speak. Every name I couldn't recall, every item I forgot to get at the supermarket. Recently, for example, I drove home from the shopping mall and turned down every wrong street. I knew it was because I was distracted (I should have been at home writing this book, not shopping for things I didn't need!), and not because my brain was starting to succumb to a disease that I may not even get—but the seed of doubt was there. I find myself questioning such incidents on a regular basis, even though my family history may not even be physically relevant.

How do you receive such a diagnosis and not let it consume you? Is it selfish to not want to know? Should you use that information to help pave the way for your family's future without you? And if you did find out, would you tell your family and friends?

Putting the emotional toll aside, that kind of information on a medical database somewhere could potentially have huge ramifications. Would your employer be interested in knowing that at some point down the track you could start to make mistakes that might impact the business? Would a health insurer or life-insurance company classify it as a 'pre-existing condition'?

In Australia you are required by law to inform your local licensing authority of any medical condition that may affect your ability to drive. Dementia is one of those conditions. Before a valid licence is issued, you need to be assessed by a doctor and, based on the results, the licensing authority will decide whether you can continue to drive for the next twelve months, after which time you need to be reassessed. They can also place certain restrictions on your licence, such as only driving within a certain vicinity of home, at certain times, or below a particular speed limit. If you cause an accident and haven't disclosed a diagnosis of Alzheimer's or dementia, you can be charged with a driving offence, or even sued—and your insurance company is unlikely to cover you for the accident.

The Alzheimer's Australia website lists several signs that dementia may be affecting a person's driving—obvious ones to do with vision, hearing, reaction time and coordination. Then it asks questions like 'Are they able to stay in the correct lane? Can they read a road map and follow detour notes? Has their mood changed when driving, from calm to angry or aggressive?' Judging from those last few, my husband is further down this Alzheimer's track than I am. Of course I am joking (except on the road map one—and then on some days the calm to angry one). There is quite a lot of information about how Alzheimer's and dementia can affect certain legal situations; if you are in doubt about yourself or a loved one, it is worth a search online. There are links in the back of this book but as laws differ from state to state it is advisable to download your local rules and regulations.

So, knowing you are likely to succumb to this disease is a double-edged sword. It's certainly not something you would post on a dating website.

This may be the appropriate time to lay some statistics down. Warning: these figures could cause you to run screaming from the room in a 'Holy shit, we are all doomed!' kind of way. But keep in mind there is wonderful research being done around Alzheimer's and dementia—so a cure could be within our generation's lifetime.

These statistics from Alzheimer's Australia were current to February 2016.

- Alzheimer's disease is the most common form of dementia, affecting up to 70 per cent of all people with dementia.

- There are no official numbers, as many people live with dementia and are not diagnosed—especially when it comes to people under the age of 65.
- Worldwide, there are more than 46.8 million people diagnosed with dementia today and 131.5 million predicted by 2050.
- In Australia, 353,800 people are estimated to be living with dementia. This figure is expected to rise to 400,000 in less than five years. Given that these figures are based on people with an 'official' diagnosis, the true number could be significantly higher—especially in those under the age of 65.
- Each week in Australia, there are more than 1800 new cases of dementia (approximately one person every six minutes).
- Dementia affects almost three in ten people over the age of 85; and almost one in ten people over the age of 65; 'younger-onset dementia' affects about 25,100 Australians under the age of 65.
- More than 50 per cent of residents in Australian government–subsidised aged care facilities have dementia.
- An estimated 1.2 million people are involved in the care of a person with dementia.
- Dementia is the second leading cause of death in Australia.

If that doesn't scare the crap out of you, I'm not sure what will.

Recent surveys indicate that contracting Alzheimer's is in the top five issues Australians worry about on a daily basis.

Nice to know I'm not alone here—or is it?

10

Let the games begin

It's almost undeniable that Alzheimer's is harder on family and friends than the person who actually has it. If you have spent any time at all in a dementia ward, it quickly becomes evident that many of the residents are existing in their own worlds and going about their business, unaware of the upheaval around them—and sometimes that can be comforting, however insensitive this may sound. Amidst all the activity, the scenes that unfold in dementia wards every day can range from depressing, to hilarious, to downright scary, and many of our visits to Mum were not that far removed from *One Flew Over the Cuckoo's Nest*.

Given that Dad spent most of his time in Mum's dementia ward, he knew the dispositions of just about every person in residence. One of the first residents he encountered was 'The

'Whistler'. Obviously I won't be using real names in this book, to protect the identity and the dignity of these wonderful people; I'm not sure Dad actually knew this particular gentleman's name anyway—he just called him The Whistler. (Dad isn't great with names, and never has been. Like many older Aussie males, he just calls every man 'buddy', 'matey' and 'pal', and every woman 'love', 'darl' or 'young lady'. As a child I was always 'fairy floss', but I'm pretty sure he just liked calling me that and hadn't actually forgotten my name.)

The Whistler walked around the dementia ward whistling all day. Well, it wasn't really a whistle as such—more like the noise you make when you suck in air and it makes a bit of a whistling sound. A bit like the noise someone who can't whistle makes when they're trying to whistle for their dog, or to get someone's attention. Just a really annoying kind of noise.

According to Dad, The Whistler only really whistled to 'get on your mum's goat'. Imagine that: here was a man, being cared for in a dementia ward, who walked around all day whistling, and he only did it to annoy, specifically, my mother. I tried explaining to Dad, who was never very tolerant of 'general weirdness' in any case, that The Whistler probably didn't even realise he was whistling at all—but he'd have none of that. 'He bloody knows alright!' Dad would fume.

To make matters worse, it transpired that The Whistler was also a bit of a kleptomaniac. A few weeks after she was admitted, I bought Mum a few pairs of new trousers and left them in a bag on her bed. Later that afternoon, Dad saw The

Whistler walking by with the said bag tucked securely under his arm. Dad mentioned it to one of the carers, who then proceeded to approach the alleged felon with caution, as he did tend to have a bit of a violent streak. The Whistler took off like the clappers. It took three carers to chase him down and procure the bag, which weighed suspiciously more than a few pairs of trousers should. When Dad took the bag back to Mum's room and emptied it onto Mum's bed, he discovered that The Whistler had also taken two picture frames, a half-eaten box of jellies, a number of DVDs (all possibly André Rieu), the remote control from the DVD player and a bottle of moisturiser.

The stolen goods were never in any danger of actually leaving the building, as security was taken very seriously. The doors at every entrance were locked with security codes to ensure the residents couldn't just wander off. Obtaining entry could be a challenge—like walking into a butterfly enclosure at the zoo. As soon as a door opens, there are usually a few people gathered waiting for their chance at freedom; you really have to slip in through the slimmest of cracks so as not to let anyone out. One woman on Mum's floor used to sit inside by the entrance with her legs across the doorway, so that whenever anyone pushed the door open, she'd be alerted to any possible opportunity for an early release. Dad got into the habit, whenever he heard the security code disarming on the other side of the door, of calling out 'Legs, legs, legs!' by way of warning as the unsuspecting visitor went to push open the door. Leaving was also an exercise in deception. If you lingered at the door to say goodbye, by the time your hand was reaching for the keypad there'd usually be a few hangers-on ready to leave with you. There was no point in trying to slip out with them all gathered there or you'd spend the next five minutes trying to push bodily extremities and limbs back inside—like trying to push a blob of Silly Putty back into its tin. Instead, you had to plan a few steps ahead, say goodbye discreetly nowhere near the exit, pretend you were heading in one direction—and then make a run for the door.

There was one woman who was always beautifully dressed, hair impeccably groomed, who walked around the nursing home with an air of grace and elegance. I'm not sure if Alzheimer's and dementia patients have a 'look' about them, but this particular lady didn't fit the norm. So much so that based on her appearance alone, she managed to wander out of the secure facility several times each week. As visitors would leave, she would swan up to them at the door and, with a straightening of her twin set, exit the building.

Having said all that, a few weeks after the great trouser robbery, I did see The Whistler leave the ward with a family member for the day, and he did actually have a couple of bags tucked under his arm. So maybe he *did* 'bloody know alright!'

One afternoon, shortly after Dad had fed Mum her lunch in the dining area, he headed back to her room to grab a snack for himself. When he opened the door, the room was darkened, with the blind down and the curtains drawn. As

he stepped inside he was greeted with a chirpy 'Good afternoon', but could barely make out the shape of a lady sitting
on Mum's couch. Each step further inside was met with a
crunching sound from under his feet. He switched the light
on to see Doris from next door sitting comfortably on the
couch, munching her way through a big box of chocolates
perched on her lap—tossing each empty wrapper on the floor
in front of her. As he moved closer to take the box from Doris,
she graciously held up the almost empty box and asked if he
would like one. How generous of Doris to offer Dad one of the
last chocolates from a box that belonged to my mum, while
sitting on Mum's couch in Mum's room! But these weren't
just any old chocolates from the supermarket. No, they were
a box of American See's Candies—a hot commodity in our
family. Every single chocolate in that box was a winner, and
I had brought that box back especially for Mum on my last
trip to the United States. Ordinarily that would have been
the kind of story Dad would have relayed to me during our
nightly phone call, but oddly enough I didn't hear about that
particular incident until quite a few years later. Perhaps he
feared the wrath I would have laid upon Doris for eating those
chocolates—we all have our Achilles heels, don't we? Good
decision, Dad.

There was another resident in Mum's ward who was gifted
with—shall we say—light fingers. Rosa was a delightful elderly
lady who always had a smile on her face. She took a liking to
my baby son, often greeting him with a double cheek squeeze

and a heartfelt 'Bellissimo, bambino!' But the lovely Rosa had a dark side. She would wander through the dining room at meal times smiling at everyone, waving and chatting . . . and then as soon as someone looked away—swoop! As fast as lightning she would steal something from their dinner plate. It didn't seem to matter what was on the menu; Rosa just had an appetite for other people's food. Given that one of the toughest jobs for the carers is getting the residents to eat, maybe Rosa thought she was doing the residents a favour: a clean plate was always met with praise, and Rosa was just helping everyone along. A few of the residents were onto her and would brace themselves for the incoming invasion—but for the most part she had a pretty successful strike rate. My dad was there for every meal my mother consumed throughout her entire stay at the nursing home, so she never made it past him. I could see Dad tense up whenever Rosa started her meal-time rounds, and he'd defend Mum's plate like a lioness defends her cubs. As Rosa's hand reached out, he would attempt to stab it with Mum's fork. I chastised him on many occasions, pointing out that he could do some real damage if he actually made contact with her hand and that Rosa probably didn't understand that her actions were distressing to him. 'Teach her a bloody lesson!' he'd retort. Most diners, however, didn't put up a fight. They all thought they were doing a good job of finishing their meal—even if they couldn't remember eating those last two potatoes.

My aunt—Mum's sister—was quite the procurer during her time spent as a resident in a nursing home too. One afternoon when my cousin was visiting, she noticed her wearing new reading glasses. Being the primary carer outside the nursing home, my cousin was pretty much across everything that my aunt had in her possession, so she enquired where the new specs had come from. My aunt replied that they'd been given to her by a fellow resident, as she couldn't seem to locate her original pair. A few days later, my aunt was wearing an entirely different set of glasses. Same question received the same answer—she'd been given these even newer glasses by a fellow resident. A quick hunt around my aunt's room revealed no signs of her original glasses, nor the pair she had been given the week before. During her next visit, my cousin arrived to find her mum with no glasses at all. When asked where they were, my aunt replied, 'Somebody has stolen them.' My cousin had just about had enough of the great glasses saga and decided it was time for a thorough search of my aunt's room. When you have a loved one with Alzheimer's or dementia, you need to think like they would in order to get to the bottom of situations like this, so my cousin pulled out every drawer and every box in every cupboard in my aunt's room—and there, piled up at the back of the sock drawer, were over a dozen pairs of reading glasses. She gathered them up in a bag and took them out into the communal area, hoping to return each pair to their rightful owner. What unfolded was a scene not dissimilar to a food drop in a famine-ravaged country.

Hands swooped in from everywhere, grabbing whatever they could—one woman walked away with three pairs, and it turned out she didn't even wear glasses! My cousin had her own reading glasses ripped from her face during the ordeal and had to pry them out of the hands of a woman who truly believed they were hers.

To this day, I don't think Dad totally accepts that people with Alzheimer's or dementia do not have total control over their actions, and I found this one of the toughest things to deal with. Even after sitting with Mum day in, day out in that ward, he still had this belief in the back of his mind that the people in her ward were capable of making the right decisions. Call it denial or false hope, but he always talked about Mum as if she still had days of utter lucidness. Occasionally during our nightly phone call he would say she'd had a good day and 'was chatting away like a merry magpie', but from spending so much time with Mum during those final six years of her life, I know that barely a word came out of her mouth—and certainly for the last three to four years she was totally non-verbal. So as much as I wanted to snap him into reality, it became painfully obvious that he needed to continue with that facade. Whether it made him feel better, or was his way of protecting us from reality, it got him through—and who was I to take that away from him?

11

Clothing optional

Alzheimer's robs its sufferers of many things, but none more unkind than dignity. You hear so many stories of wild goings-on in dementia wards—patients in bed with each other, everyone running around naked, like scenes from *The Benny Hill Show*. (Now I have that 'Yakety Sax' music in my head. Google it, and then good luck trying to get it out of your head for the rest of the day.) I didn't actually see much of that action within Mum's facility, thank goodness, but I do think a good story sometimes gets in the way of the facts.

Alfie was the closest we got to such shenanigans.

Alfie liked to walk; in fact he walked around and around the ward all day. (Interesting fact: many dementia wards are designed in a layout that makes it easy for the residents to walk around. Mum's facility, for example, had the rooms on the outside of the corridors, and a circular courtyard in the middle.) When I'd be there visiting Mum, Alfie would probably walk past about thirty times. Nothing unusual about that, except that his state of dress—or should I say *undress*—seemed to change every few passes. I was sitting there one day with my niece, who was probably around 25 at the time, and Alfie walked past just wearing a white singlet. Not being a seasoned visitor, she commented how embarrassing it was to see an older gentleman's private parts. Dad replied, 'At least he's wearing a bloody singlet.'

At any given time, a number of residents would be walking around in various states of dress and undress—you just got used to it.

The dress code in dementia wards seems to range from decent to anything that happens to be lying on anybody else's bed. All clothing must be labelled so the laundry service knows which room to deliver the fresh clothes to. Not that it made much difference—I would often spot another resident strolling around in Mum's nice cardigan or lovely fluffy dressing gown. It wasn't a big deal in the scheme of things, as we usually got those items back after the next laundry day, but if most houses have a 'sock heaven', then most dementia wards must have *many* heavens, for every piece of clothing conceivable. And when it comes to underpants—that's not even worth arguing about. Once they have been relocated, there is no return neccessary, thanks very much.

After a while you become savvy to the clothing etiquette. Anything that you want kept exclusively for use by your loved one on a particular occasion—say a birthday lunch or Christmas Day—then best you bring that item in on the day, dress your loved one, then kiss that bejewelled piece of clothing goodbye. The more it sparkles, the more attractive it is lying on the bed or in a laundry hamper.

Push walkers are another hot commodity. Mum's walker would often go missing and we'd have to search high and low for it. Usually we'd find it sitting in Elsie's room around the corner—Elsie sometimes had up to three walkers jammed into her comfy little abode. She would head off for a walk and just pick up the first walker she saw along the way. (Maybe nursing homes should consider a system like they have for bicycles in cities, where you can pick up a bike, ride it around, then drop it off at various locations around town.) The recovery of a walker was often met with hostility, but Dad became quite adept at taking corners, pushing at full speed.

Most walkers were decorated with knick-knacks that had personal meaning to the residents. In Mum's ward, football teams were quite the thing in terms of push-walker bling. Mum was a diehard Collingwood fan (if you don't know much about AFL, all you really need to know is that if you don't barrack for Collingwood, then you despise them), but we decided against adopting their black and white team colours on Mum's walker, thinking that anything that may cause aggression might not be a good thing. Some people take this walker decoration bizzo very seriously—get a line of residents walking to the dining room at meal time and the procession can look like a Moomba Parade. (For non-Victorian readers, replace Moomba with Mardi Gras, but with fewer tits and feathers and rainbows. I may have just stumbled onto an idea for a new reality show: *Pimp My Walker!*)

There was always something happening at Mum's dementia ward. Trevor was another resident pacer—but he didn't just pace, he paced with a purpose. Trevor would trot past numerous times during our visits, sometimes pushing a walking frame in front of him (suspiciously not his, as the one he favoured always had some knitting in the front basket). Round and round he would go, passing us every few minutes—each pass met with a friendly hello. Next pass he would have a different walker. Next an empty wheelchair. Next the laundry trolley, food trolley, a pram from the 'nursery' set up in one of the common areas. Personally, I enjoyed it when he came past pushing one of the other inmates in their wheelchair—usually with the passenger screaming in protest. Trevor could get up an impressive speed when he committed to it, so it was quite a job to ensure the path of his circuit remained clear, as he didn't stop for anything or anybody.

I guess there really isn't much to do in these wards day in, day out. Visitors are welcomed with open arms, and over time everyone starts to look out for each others' loved ones; amazing bonds are formed with strangers who are going through the same experiences. Nobody is judgemental of other patients or their families, and they tend to take on the care of those who don't have friends and family coming in to visit. Dad was there every single day, all day, so he became a familiar face, and took on an enormous amount of responsibility. We would often arrive to see him wandering around the corridors with an old lady, other than my mother, on his arm.

Gladys took a particular shine to Dad. She would follow him around all day and night. In a way it was lucky Mum wasn't with it enough to notice, or it might have been on for young and old. Our family would roll in on a Sunday for morning tea—sometimes eight of us at a time—then position chairs around the communal living area and lay out muffins and cakes on the coffee tables; Gladys would bring a chair over and settle in for the family gathering. The only trouble was, while Gladys loved Dad, she wasn't fond of many other people. If anyone came within cooee of him, she would push them away, or start swinging her arms and yelling at them. Gladys would have tipped the scales at around 45 kilos, but get an old woman on a mission and she can definitely punch above her weight. God help anyone if they sat next to Dad in an empty chair while Gladys was off doing something else. She would literally drag them out of the chair, hurling abuse colourfully sprinkled with profanity. And if Gladys couldn't find Dad, she would wander around the corridors calling his name, wandering into rooms looking for him; I would sometimes arrive and find Dad hiding out in Mum's darkened room, with the door locked. When Dad would leave the ward at night, Gladys would make her way to the balcony overlooking the car park and stand there waving until he was out of sight. It was all rather heartwarming to some degree, but I imagine it took a bit of a toll on him, and more frustratingly for him, started to impact upon his ability to care for Mum in the way he wanted to. Eventually Gladys's affection wavered—probably helped by the fact that Dad would constantly try to redirect her affections to any other male within a one-mile radius.

Love can be fickle in dementia wards. I've seen devoted husbands and wives spend endless amounts of time caring for their partners, and not receive even a glimmer of recognition from the person they have spent most of their lives with. I can't imagine what that would be like. I experienced it as a daughter, having spent years with my mother looking blankly at me, without any sense of knowing who I was—but to have your lifelong partner look at you like that must be soul destroying.

I recently watched a BBC documentary by Louis Theroux called *Extreme Love: Dementia* about a couple in their early fifties who'd been together since high school and had a nine-year-old daughter; the woman who was diagnosed with Alzheimer's on her forty-seventh birthday was getting to the point of needing full-time care in a dementia ward. The husband confided that he was already starting to think about the future without his wife, and that once she was being cared for full time in a facility and had lost the ability to recognise him or their daughter, he would probably file for divorce and start forging a new life for them.

Wow. That hit me hard. Given that I am 50, and have a young son, and potentially have that black cloud hanging over my head—how would I feel about that?

I guess most of us would want to say that, in the same situation, we would absolutely want our family to move on and be happy without us. Mum used the 'lock me up and throw away the key' line many times—and for at least the last six years of her life she had no idea who any of us were. She wasn't aware of the birth of my only son, now seven, who she most desperately wanted me to have. She wasn't aware that my brother's kids have all grown up into wonderful human beings. She wasn't aware that my sister has become a successful businesswoman who has just built her own house. And I doubt she was aware that Dad sat next to her, holding her hand, every single day from sun up to sun down, while she sat in that nursing home, basically just existing.

At least, I don't think she knew any of that.

It's a horrible situation to be faced with, and there are no wrong or right ways of dealing with the impact of losing someone to this disease before their time. I guess that is the reason so many patients exist in their facilities without any visits from family or friends. It comes to a point where some families decide that life goes on. For them, moving on is the best way forward, knowing their loved one is being cared for in the best way possible by staff who see and experience first hand more than most of us would have to endure in a lifetime.

I have had this conversation with my husband. If I do develop Alzheimer's and am at the point of not recognising him or my son—then move on.

Just don't move on with certain people from the list of women I have provided, mainly my girlfriends and his ex-girlfriends. Oh, and there's a list of songs they can't play at their wedding . . . and a list of places they can't visit together.

I think that's fair, isn't it?

Mum's mother and father—
Barney and Alma—standing
outside their house in
Collingwood, c. 1950.

Mum (Beverley Alma Pitt) aged
three and a half months, in
February, 1936.

Mum and Dad on the night of their engagement in 1954. I love this photo:
so classically beautiful and innocent.

Mum and Dad on
their wedding day,
8 October 1955.

Mum on the honeymoon somewhere in Adelaide. Nothing says newlywed like a nice piece of road kill.

My Nana enjoying the Christmas festivities in the world's biggest chair.

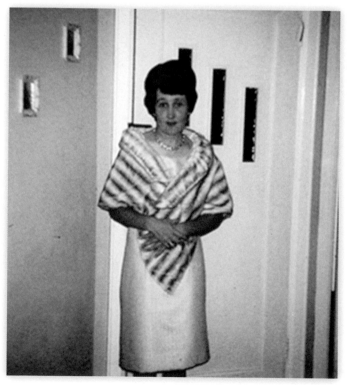

Mum all dolled up for a night out, in the doorway of our family home c. 1960.

Mum and I strike a beach pose.

The playpen my parents used to put me in while the rest of the family enjoyed a day at the beach. Either I was not the smartest kid, or they figured those legs wouldn't carry me far away as they didn't bother to use the fourth side of the enclosure.

The three kids: my brother Peter, my sister Jenni and me. I'm the one who has clearly fallen down the crack of the couch.

The three kids again. With colour photography also came better photo composition.

Me amid the Christmas morning present frenzy. I later found that Hands Down board game in the back of the garage when we cleaned out the family home forty years later.

My sister Jenni and me on the backyard swingset, wearing homemade dresses (and judging from my sister, homemade haircuts too).

My sister and me modelling the latest homemade fashions of the early seventies. Mum obviously anticipated me growing like a weed with the size of that hem.

As a going-away gift, Mum presented my sister and me with these hand-painted Aussie-themed windcheaters for our backpacking tour around Europe in 1988. I'm the cockatoo and Jenni's the koala.

Mum and Dad, always the life of the party, dancing together at my brother's wedding.

Mum's fiftieth birthday. Dad tearing up the dance floor in usual style and Mum looking embarrassed, also in usual style. Look up the term 'daggy dad dancing' and I'm pretty sure you will a picture of Frankie.

Mum and Dad at the Grand Canyon. On one of their trips over to visit me while I was living in Los Angeles, the three of us went on a two-week road trip through the west coast of the United States.

Mum and Dad at the Statue of Liberty. This was taken on a trip to visit me while I was living in New York City. This is their own version of the obligatory holding-up-the-Leaning-Tower-of-Pisa tourist snap.

The family at my twenty-first birthday. From left to right, my sister Jenni, my brother Peter, Dad, me and Mum.

Mum and her sister Desma in their usual state—non-stop talking—while Dad sits silently in the background, smiling.

Dad and I always insisted on dragging Mum into photo booths. She was never a big fan of having her photo taken, which made this even more fun.

Mum, Dad and me on my wedding day. This photo was taken just after the ceremony had taken place in the lounge room of my husband's parents house in Camas, Washington. The carpenter who was building their deck just happened to be a minister so he performed the official duties.

Dad hamming it up for the camera. Getting a serious shot of him has never been easy. I had just cut his hair with the dog clippers so he gathered up all of the clippings and placed them on his head to make it look like he had more hair.

Mum and Dad proudly showing off their orchids in one of their three greenhouses in the backyard. The family pool was torn down the day after I moved out to make way for more orchids.

This photo of Mum was taken the Christmas of the cookie baking incident. Little did we know this would be the last Christmas we would spend with our mum as we knew her.

This was taken the Christmas after her diagnosis, the last in the family home. You can see she has very red eyes and has a handkerchief in her lap. The constant crying and pacing had started by then. And of course there is Dad putting on the brave face for us all.

Dad showing Mum our newborn son, Sam. Mum was in the nursing home by this stage and I'm pretty certain she never really knew that this was her grandson.

Grandparents are Special

ave Pa and Nanna. They live far away from us. I play with Pa
cause he is very funny, because he tries to make me laugh. I don't do
thing with Nanna 'cos she's sick. I love them 20 inches long.'
n 27/5

My son Sam was asked at school to do a drawing of his grandparents and what they meant to him. The picture features Pa standing in the middle and then Nan on the right, just hovering out of her wheelchair. His text reads: 'Grandparents are special. I have Pa and Nanna. They live far away from us. I play with Pa because he is very funny, because he tries to make me laugh. I don't do anything with Nanna 'cos she's sick. I love them 20 inches long.'

My awesome family together in February 2015. From left to right, my sister Jenni, me, my brother Peter and Dad.

Me and my hero—my gorgeous dad—in 2015.

Me with the the lights of my life:
husband Ed and our beautiful
son Sam (aged 7).

12

Take my wife

Given that many dementia wards and nursing homes are inhabited by the elderly, you often see couples who have been admitted together. Quite often, one is in a worse state than the other, but keeping them together seems to be the best option, and perhaps less disorienting for them.

During the course of Mum's stay, we saw quite a few couples come and go—one couple in particular, Gwen and Len (even their names were a match made in heaven). In terms of their level of awareness, Gwen and Len were fairly evenly paired; quite simply, they were under the impression that they'd been checked into some swanky hotel. A hotel in which everything you could ever want was provided, and the staff were very helpful and attentive. I would see them each time I visited, wandering around the corridors hand in hand, having a lovely time on their 'holiday'. Always pleasant, with big smiles and warm greetings. Numerous times during the course of a visit I would receive a 'Nice to meet you' and 'Isn't this a lovely place?'

The beautiful thing about seeing them in that nursing home was that everyone was happy to play along with them, to keep Gwen and Len in their happy place. Could you imagine Gwen and Len out in the wide world? They'd be a pair of sitting ducks. You hear stories of people taking advantage of the elderly and swindling them out of their life savings—and without the safe haven of that nursing home, Gwen and Len would surely have fallen victim to some dodgy individual who saw an opportunity to make a quick buck. But instead, they happily coexisted in their five-star resort, enjoying comfortable accommodation, three delicious meals a day, a laundry service, movie night, and staff on hand 24/7 to assist them with anything they needed to make their stay more comfortable. The only time I saw the downside of this scenario was when Gwen sidled up to me one morning and asked what time check-out was, as they were heading home that day. In fact, Gwen started to ask me that question quite a bit towards the end of their 'holiday'.

There was another lovely old couple that I started noticing around the ward—always hand in hand, and seemingly both happily slipping into old age together. I took a minute to chat with one of the carers, to gain some insight into their life together and how they'd wound up there. The carer responded rather matter-of-factly that they weren't in fact a couple, but single patients who *thought* they were a couple, and spent their days existing within that belief. Part of me was astonished, but then I also thought it was a lovely thing to have happened to them both. If it meant they were living happily in a world that brought them comfort, then why not. Can you imagine what it will be like when the young adults of today are populating nursing homes. Their Tinder apps will be getting quite the workout.

The same Louis Theroux documentary also followed a storyline of a man aged in his late sixties who had been admitted to a dementia ward by his wife, who could no longer care for him at home. He was physically fit and active, but in his mind he was back in his thirties—a successful dentist, and still quite the ladies man. His wife visited him every day, but he would continually introduce women to her as his 'new girlfriend'. One woman in particular spent quite a bit of time with him, and his wife would have to sit through these visits feeling like 'the third wheel'. When carers would try to explain to him that the visiting woman was actually his wife, he would become confused and upset. As devoted as she was to her husband, she admitted it was almost time to sever ties and move on with her own life—she found no reason to put herself or her husband through the torment of daily visits.

It's a tough road to hoe—keeping up a premise that is false, even for the sake of someone's happiness. There are different schools of thought on how to manage the fine line between fact and fiction in these situations. How do you deal with questions that might lead to an answer an Alzheimer's sufferer really doesn't want to hear—such as when someone with Alzheimer's asks after a loved one who has already died? Do you pretend that the person they are asking after is alive and well and will visit them soon, or do you 'remind' them that their loved one has already passed on?

One technique I heard about for caring for loved ones with Alzheimer's was being trialled in a facility in the United States. Carers would write down key facts about a patient's life on a small notepad, which was kept with the patient at all times. When the carers were asked a question like 'Where is my wife?', the patient was asked to look at their notepad and read what was written down. In one particular case, an elderly gentleman kept asking after his wife who had died many years before. On his notepad, the carers had written, 'Katherine passed away fifteen years ago and is now resting in heaven.' Every time this gentleman pulled out his notepad and read that sentence, he would break down and cry. The carers would talk him through the initial shock, but then get him focused again, and he would go about his business quite happily until the next time he asked after his dearly departed Katherine. Such grief time after time must have been excruciating to see, but I guess they'd done enough work with him, and enough research on this technique, to conclude this was the best way to deal with that constant question.

My friend's grandmother, who had Alzheimer's, would also frequently ask after her husband, who had died many years before. The family chose to respond to that question with, 'He has just gone down the shops, Nan, and will be back later.' As a family, they had decided that a little white lie was the best way to deal with their nan—and that worked for them.

Different horses for different courses.

Another question frequently asked—as with the afore-mentioned Gwen and Len—is, 'When am I going home?' I saw many families leave Mum's nursing home in distress, with their loved one at the door wailing and pleading to be taken home.

I know how awful it feels to leave a young child at day care; my son would be clinging to my leg, begging me not to leave. The teacher would always tell me to use the 'band-aid method'—a quick rip, detach and walk away as fast as you can. Short-term pain for long-term gain. I knew that five minutes down the road my son had forgotten how much he missed me, and how much he resented me leaving him there, and was happily playing with his friends—but I was often driving to work in tears, left fragile and scarred by the morning's events. Walking away from a loved one upset by being left behind at the nursing home is perhaps similar in some ways; I'm just not sure how many patients are happily playing Lego with their friends five minutes after you've left.

We never had that issue with Mum, as she became rather non-verbal quite early on. Knowing my mother, she would've asked after her beloved football team—and I would happily have told her over and over again that they were doing well, sitting on top of the ladder, and would without a doubt win the premiership that season. A little white lie wouldn't have hurt in that situation, surely—especially given her team's form over those last few years. Hey, I might have even started believing it myself.

As weird and selfish as it sounds, I am sometimes thankful Mum was non-verbal. We never had to endure the questions and the protests that I saw on a daily basis with other families. It's heartbreaking, and there is no wrong or right way to deal with such situations. You just have to do what works for you—and whatever works at that particular moment to get you through.

13

Baby talk

My son spent the first five years of his life visiting his nana in the nursing home. Talk about valuable life lessons: they don't come more valuable than that. There is something very comforting and endearing about watching my son—now seven years old—walk up to strangers in wheelchairs in shopping centres and say hello. He doesn't seek them out in a creepy kind of way, but he finds nothing odd about seeing someone wheel past him. Even if that person looks different to him, or sounds different to him, he sees them as just what they are: a human being. Kids generally are very accepting of people, no matter what they look like, but I honestly feel he is a better kid for all his visits to Nana's nursing home. He never saw her out of her chair or wheelchair—that's just how she was. When his class at school were asked to draw a picture of their grandparents for Grandparents Day, my son arrived home with his drawing (which is in the picture section). It showed a pretty good likeness of Pa, standing on the left, with Nana in her wheelchair on the right. He wrote, 'My papa is funny and I like playing with him. I can't play with my nana because she is sick. I love them 20 inches long.'

He never had to experience a crazy nana, like I did. One of my last memories of my own nan was visiting her in hospital when I was about eleven, a few weeks before she passed away. I walked through a ward past what seemed like hundreds of beds (quite likely around a dozen) and found Nana's bed towards the back of the room on the right. She was tucked in under some white sheets, looking very frail, but also very peaceful. I sidled up to get a closer look, and as my hand touched hers she lifted her head off the pillow. I waited for that familiar smile that only a nana can give to her youngest granddaughter. She opened her eyes, looked at me, put her hand on mine and whispered, 'Don't go near that cupboard behind you, because there is a man in there that will come out and take you away.' Holy shit, Nan! I knew she was a bit crazy and had a bad memory, but WTF? She's talking like someone who writes for Wes Craven films.

I had always looked on the positive side of Nan being a bit nuts. She always said funny things, and she gave the best presents—some of which may have been obtained using less than conventional methods. My cousins often received expensive bottles of perfume for birthdays and Christmas, and when asked how she could afford such extravagance, Nan would claim they only cost around $1.50 each. A few different theories have gone around our family over the years as to how Nana came into such good fortune with her shopping. She'd spent so much time in department stores in the city that maybe some of the proprietors looked fondly upon her and gave her merchandise at a ridiculously discounted rate? Another theory is that she had a secret stash of money hidden away and would use it buy us expensive gifts and claim they had cost next to nothing. And then there is the obvious theory, which probably doesn't need explaining. As a kid I just remember the cool gifts—who cared how she got them.

Having someone in your life who suffers from dementia can be confronting, especially if you are a child, but it also instils in you a good level of acceptance. When we visited Mum, my son spent most of the time playing with his cars on the floor, showing her his latest acquisition. He didn't question the fact that Nana never responded—that's just how she was. One morning a carer walked past and saw him hold up something to show his nana. The carer asked him if he was having a nice visit with his nana. He was. She then asked him what Nana thought of his new car. He looked at me, then at his dad, then at Nana, back at me, then looked to the carer and said, 'Nana can't speak.' There it is, plain and simple. Nana can't speak, and that wasn't in the least bit odd to him.

On another visit, Mum had spent most of the time asleep in her chair, as she regularly did; our visits were more about being there than actually interacting with her, as she was often asleep, especially towards the end. I was sitting in a chair next to her, reading the paper. My son was playing on an iPad. One of the other visitors walked past and stopped to chat with us, and asked him how Nana was doing today. He looked up from his iPad to his nana semi-slumped in her chair. 'She's dead,' he answered, and went back to playing his game. The woman gasped, so I quickly tried to reassure them both that Nana wasn't dead, but merely sleeping. He looked up at his nana again and said, 'Nup, she's dead,' then back to his iPad. I wasn't sure what the right thing to do would've been, but I'm pretty sure I didn't do it. I leant over to Mum, picked up her arm and started waving it around, saying, 'Look! I'm not dead, I'm not dead, I'm just sleeping!' in a *Weekend at Bernie's* kind of way. My son ignored me, and the nice lady who had kindly stopped to visit quickly beat a hasty retreat.

As well as the awkward moments, there are also the heart-warming ones that come with taking children into nursing homes. Entering the building with a baby is like walking down the street with an eight-week-old labrador puppy: everybody wants a piece. My son's cheeks were squeezed so often they were permanently red from the age of one month to three years. The presence of a baby or toddler did amazing things to the overall mood within the building. I would walk around with my son, holding him in front of me like he was a fine bottle of wine being presented to a table in a five-star restaurant. While he was a baby I was quite strict about not letting the patients hold him, but as he started walking, he would often disappear down the corridor on the end of a relatively strange elderly hand, which he knew was safe enough to do within the circular confines of the dementia ward. Once he got a little older, he turned his hand to helping out with the therapy games. Keep the balloon in the air, catch and throw the ball, knock down the plastic bowling pins, and his all-time favourite—quoits. It was just like a kids' party, except less sugar and much less running around in capes and tutus.

After Mum passed, I didn't have much cause to take my son back to the nursing home, but during the last school holidays, we visited Dad for lunch. As Dad still spends quite a bit of time there, and quite a bit of effort on the gardens, he wanted to show my son around the grounds and the vegie plot he'd recently planted. So we arrived at the nursing home, popped the four-digit code into the keypad, and instantly were transported back in time. The memories came flooding back, and I felt myself getting rather emotional. As we were walking through to the communal dining area, we noticed a gentleman seated at a table on his own. My son waved as we walked past, and the man started shouting 'Hey, hey, hey, hey!' over and over again, at a ridiculously loud volume, snapping me out of my Hallmark moment. My son didn't miss a beat—he smiled at the gentleman and kept on walking.

Dad was in his element showing his grandson around the garden, in the process picking up all the fruit and flowers lying along the path, muttering 'Bloody pests!' with every bloom he picked up, cursing the pesky residents who took it upon themselves to prematurely prune and harvest.

After pottering around the garden for a while, we started to head towards the door leading back into the living area. We noticed a group of ladies being led through the room into the games area, ready to start an activity. Dad's protective instincts kicked in, and he grabbed my son before I could open the door, suggesting we wait until the passing parade had finished. I had faith in my boy's ability to cope with a bunch of old ladies, so I brazenly flung open the door and pushed him forward into the room. It was like a band member of One Direction had just turned up at the local school prom: arms and faces were coming at him at a rapid pace—grabbing him, kissing him, patting him on the head. I watched my seven-year-old stand calmly in the middle of a bunch (would the collective noun be a 'wander'?) of dementia-suffering women, smiling and nodding at them for over five minutes. One lady took a particular interest in his hair, and for the entire time ran her fingers across his forehead, brushing his fringe back over his head. He just stood there and took it; this is the same kid who won't let me near his hair when I'm trying to get him ready for school. Another woman was talking to him in Maltese, and every time she paused for an answer from him, he would look to me and I would mouth, 'Just say yes.' He would nod and say yes and she would continue talking. Every now and then the word 'spaghetti' would come out of her mouth, which piqued his interest, being a big fan of spaghetti.

The games coordinator came over to break up the party and get the 'wander' moving along in an orderly fashion to their scheduled activity. In the organised chaos, the coordinator didn't notice that she'd lost one—the Maltese lady had decided she was coming with us and proceeded to follow us to the exit, through the dining room, and past the solo diner, who again started up his 'Hey, hey, hey!' Our party of four had made it to the exit doors. Dad, in his haste to avoid the impending drama of leaving our new friend behind, couldn't quite punch in the passcode correctly. He tried it over five times, but simply wasn't pushing the buttons hard enough. By the time I punched the code in correctly, with an electronic click and a release, the Maltese lady was through the door, walking free. Maybe we were getting that big bowl of spaghetti for dinner after all.

Dad tried to walk her back through the door, but she wasn't having any part of it. Luckily the activity coordinator appeared, ushering the lady back into the safe confines of the dementia ward. I can only imagine where the rest of the activity group were by the time she made it back to the games room—the 'wander' would have scattered like a dropped bag of dry rice.

By the time we reached the car, I was an emotional wreck. Being back in the ward where I had spent so much time with Mum, and seeing my son nonchalantly interact with those women, was all too much. After a few minutes of hugs and kisses and praise for my beautiful boy, he firmly told me I was embarrassing him and that it was time to stop crying.

Roger that. All good.

And with all the good that comes from having your child spend time in a nursing home, there is bound to be some bad. There is no nice way of saying it, but germs love nursing homes. It must be impossible to stop patients spreading germs—most of them can't remember their own name, let alone the correct protocol when it comes to coughing, sneezing and hand sanitising.

There was always a silver lining to a gastro shutdown at the nursing home: it meant Dad was locked out for a few days, and he could spend some time with us. It may sound selfish, but in my mind, Mum was being cared for just fine where she was, and we got to have our dad back for a while. Whenever the name 'Dad' came up on my phone anytime prior to 8:30 p.m., it meant one of two things: either something was wrong with Mum, or the nursing home was in flu or gastro shutdown and Dad was locked out. Neither scenario was good, but the latter one was also tough for Dad as he'd worry that something horrible might happen to Mum and he wouldn't be able to protect her. On more than one occasion he tried to sneak into the building while it was in shutdown, but rules are rules, and he would end up making the pilgrimage to our house with his overnight bag packed with enough supplies for one day. Yep, he was always convinced he'd be back at the nursing home the next day—even though the shutdown almost always lasted four to seven days. During these lockout periods, his daily routine at our house was always the same. He would get up in the morning, come downstairs, and the first thing out of his mouth was: 'Can you give the nursing home a call and see if I can go back in?' Maybe he was imagining that a SWAT team from haz-chem had sanitised the place overnight, magically removing all traces of infection and potential contagion.

As great as it was to have Dad stay with us during those periods, watching him throughout the day was not dissimilar to seeing a dog tied up outside a supermarket waiting for its owner to emerge with a leg of lamb. He couldn't really relax, and every time my phone rang, he would rush over and hover next to me in case it was the nursing home calling with the all-clear.

He wasn't used to being away from Mum, but he did make it over to our house every Thursday night. He would get Mum settled in her bed around 8 p.m. and as soon as her eyelids shut, he would very carefully remove her hand from his and tiptoe out of the room. He would then call me from his mobile and just say, 'Leaving now,' and head down to his car. I would then call our local fish and chip shop, place our order by simply saying, 'Order for Frank,' which they would acknowledge and then hang up. I would set the table and wait for Dad to arrive. We had this routine down like a well-oiled machine. It was always a battle to get my son into bed on those Thursday nights, as he knew his papa was coming over and would use every inch of energy to stay out of bed and awake for his arrival. Dad would turn up, we would eat dinner, have a glass of wine, watch TV and chat for an hour, then we'd all go to bed. Next morning Dad was up with the birds, piece of toast for breakfast, and out the door to be back in time for Mum to have her breakfast. Outside of us visiting the nursing home, that was pretty much our entire interaction with Dad, but we took what we could get.

While Mum was in the nursing home, there was only one other time we had Dad for an extended period. It happened to be a Thursday night; my husband, my son and I were heading off overseas the following day, so Dad was going to break his routine and drop us at the airport by 9 a.m. the next morning. I was putting my son to bed, awaiting the 'Leaving now' call from Dad; it got to about 8.45 p.m. and still no call, which usually meant something had happened at the nursing home with another patient, which delayed getting everyone else into bed. By 9 p.m. I got a little anxious—fuelled by my son not cooperating with his bedtime routine and asking why Papa hadn't called yet. At 9.15 p.m. my mobile rang with an incoming call from the nursing home. The woman on the other end could speak just enough English to say the words 'Frank', 'fall' and 'hospital'. I jumped in the car and arrived at the emergency department in the next suburb to find Dad being lifted out of an ambulance on a stretcher. He looked like he'd just gone ten rounds with Mike Tyson—although thankfully both of his earlobes were intact.

Turns out the elevators in the nursing home had decided to take the night off, so Dad left the building via the dimly lit fire-exit stairwell. His foot tripped on the top step and he proceeded to tumble down a full flight of concrete stairs, ending up in a heap on the landing. It wasn't until one of the nursing staff entered the stairwell at the end of her shift that he was found trying unsuccessfully to get up. For an 82-year-old man, he chalked up an impressive list of injuries—broken nose, cracked rib, broken wrist, and a gash down to the bone on his forehead that has freakishly healed to resemble Harry Potter's scar.

So, looking for that silver lining again, we postponed our overseas trip and Dad came to stay with us for about two weeks while he recuperated. He was not the best patient by a long stretch. Even with his injuries, he was still keen to spend as much time as he could at the nursing home, so I would drive him up there, drop him off for a few hours and then bring him home. Much of those few hours in between I spent wandering around the local shopping mall, indulging in a little 'retail therapy'—but my self-medicating meanderings proved anything but therapeutic when we received our bank statement the following month!

14

Take me back

One of the fascinating things about Alzheimer patients is how their brain can transport them back in time, to a joyous period in their lives—such as the gentleman I mentioned in a previous chapter who believed with his whole heart that he was still an active practising dentist; comfortingly, the staff would go along with his conviction, and often ask him for random teeth checks to keep him in his 'happy place'.

Wouldn't it be nice if we could all just go back and live in the time of our lives again? Maybe that's the one nice thing the brain does for those with Alzheimer's. It says, 'Hey, I remember being deliriously happy when we were 25 years old—let's go there.' (I wish my own brain could physically take me back to a younger, better-looking and smaller dress-size me.)

During the early stages of her disease, Mum would walk around the house reliving phone conversations with her sister. Mum had always spent a lot of time on the phone—so much so that we used to joke she ought to have the telephone handset glued to her ear. (Lucky mobiles weren't around in her heyday or we would have had to mortgage the house to pay the phone bill—or she would have been repeatedly incarcerated for using a mobile while driving.)

Aside from those imaginary phone calls, we didn't see a retreat to any particular period in Mum's life—perhaps there wasn't one particular period of her life that she enjoyed more than another. She obviously loved her children and grandchildren with her whole heart, so they were always her 'happy place'.

It seems children are a trigger for Alzheimer patients; many go back to a time when they were caring for babies, which is why Mum's nursing home had an area set up as a pretend nursery with a cot, change table and dolls scattered around. And yes, they were the kind of dolls whose eyes follow you around the room at night. The older ladies in particular loved that area. They would spend hours in there rocking the dolls to sleep and dressing them in clothes. The human brain is so fascinating: these people had lost all ability to care for themselves and recognise their own loved ones, but still knew how to care for a baby. Basic human instinct is so strong, and you see it kick in over and over again within these facilities.

Somehow the ability to perform an ingrained or habitual task or activity is in our psyche, and we can't *not* do it.

Case in point, Bobby. A rotund Irishman who was always smiling, despite his confinement to a wheelchair—one of those bed-type ones that allow the patient to recline for medical reasons. Bobby had been in the nursing home as long as Mum and was a familiar face during our visits. He spoke with a fairly broad Irish accent, and was a fair way down the road with dementia, so there wasn't a lot of in-depth chatting going on. From what we could decipher from his conversations, Bobby was quite the fisherman in his day—and the fact he was in a nursing home confined to a wheelchair wasn't going to stop him doing what he loved. So all day long, Bobby would fish. He would lie back and cast out his imaginary line, watch it land, and then he would wait. And wait. And wait. Then, by either sheer luck or the fact that Bobby was indeed a talented fisherman, he would get a bite and reel in the catch of the day. This would go on for most of the day, casting out his line and reeling it back in. Carers and visitors would walk past and ask if the fish were biting—'Aye, aye,' he would reply. Bobby was happy as a clam (nice seafood simile, if I do say so myself), spending all day, every day, fishing from the comfort of his wheelchair. To see that every time I visited was rather endearing. It made me happy to think that as tough as this disease was for Bobby and his loved ones, he was in a place where he was safe, cared for and, in his mind, doing exactly what he loved to do.

Another resident who was reliving a past passion was Carlos. He was a boxer, and had all the moves—and the nose—to prove it. A shortish, round-bellied older European gent who got around in sweat pants, slip-on scuffs, socks and a singlet, he was always ready for the next round. Instead of the stock-standard hello and handshake, a greeting from Carlos always entailed him striking the boxing pose and throwing a friendly right jab towards you. This was all relatively harmless, unless you pissed Carlos off—then one of those right jabs would connect and all hell would break loose. Over the course of his stay there, his right jab unfortunately connected with a few too many of the residents, who had annoyed the otherwise placid Carlos by changing the channel on the communal television, or sitting in his favourite chair, or calling out for assistance from staff. Dad would often tell me that Carlos had got in a bit of a scuffle and he had to try to step in and break it up. Getting the dynamic right amongst patients can be a delicate balance—pretty sure Carlos's right jab was not listed as a hobby on his application form, after all—but for the safety of the other nursing home residents, Carlos was eventually relocated to another facility.

From where I stand, being a carer in a nursing home—and in particular a dementia ward—is hard work. I spent many hours at Mum's nursing home helping the other residents with meals, sitting and chatting with them, but whenever a volatile situation arose, I let the staff deal with it in the way they had been trained. These nurses and carers do an amazing job, and often for little thanks. I have seen patients physically and verbally abuse them, throw furniture at them, throw food in their face and generally treat them unjustly, but understanding that these patients are not of sound mind goes a long way to tolerating such behaviours. I personally would like to apologise for every time Dad walked up to a carer and complained that Mum's soup was cold! I have nothing but good things to say about the nursing staff who cared for Mum (and, inadvertently, Dad). Their competence and compassion were unwavering, and she couldn't have been in better hands.

It's not uncommon to see family member of patients who have passed on return to visit other patients or staff. A special bond is made when people are going through times of stress, and part of me thinks that it helps with the grieving process to return to a place that was so integral to a loved one's final years. On the other hand, I'm sure some families can't deal with those memories and prefer just to move on without looking back.

Two years after Mum left us, Dad still lives in the unit within the retirement village, and wanders over to the nursing home every day to have coffee with the staff. In those later years they were essentially his family, we often say. He still docs quite a bit of work around the place—mainly tending to the gardens, and conducting gardening classes twice a week for the residents.

As much as Dad loves them, those gardening classes are a source of frustration for him. After all, he is trying to teach basic gardening to a room full of dementia patients. Over the course of each one-hour class, the number of participants will go up or down, due to the nature of his clientele—because they just don't sit down and listen . . . and/or watch . . . and/or learn, as he'd say in his nightly rants to me. Another sign that Dad doesn't quite get that they have no real control over their state of mind.

The nursing home has a budget for these kind of activities, so at the start of each week Dad gets a tray of seedlings, a stack of small pots and some potting soil from the local nursery. During each class, he helps the participants fill the pots with soil and plant the seedlings in them. What stops the nursing home being overrun with freshly planted little pots is that one of the residents likes to go around and pick all the flowers off anything resembling a blooming plant. The first week it happened, Dad seriously suggested to me that they should set up security cameras on the balconies so the felon could be identified and brought to justice. I talked him down from that one.

Last winter, Dad tells me, was a tough one at the nursing home's communal gardens. They had planted six ornamental trees in the middle of the courtyard, and by early spring these should have been budding. He had been checking them every few days for signs of fresh spring growth, but nothing was happening. One morning, the reason became apparent when he discovered one of the patients carefully plucking every leaf and new shoot off the trees, which she had been painstakingly doing for weeks. I can only hope he didn't run at her with a pair of secateurs, waving and shooing her away like some crazy man—not that he would've looked odd in that particular setting, if you know what I mean. Maybe I should be enlisting this lady's services in my front garden. During summer I can't walk down my front path without being greeted by a swarm of bees inhabiting my blossom tree. No harm would come to the bees, just merely a forced relocation to the lovely blossom down the road. I would promise to visit them on my own terms. And it would be a bit of plucking therapy for the good lady picker. Everybody wins. I did hear a rumour that she grew up in India on a tea plantation, and spent much of her life picking tea leaves.

Well, it makes a good story, anyhow.

15

André, André, André

We all know the effect music can have on our memory—hearing a song on the radio or in a shopping centre can cause all kinds of memories to come flooding back, and even change our mood. A few songs can bring me to tears within the first few bars of hearing them—but I'm quite an emotional person, so that doesn't take much. I was quite close to my uncle, and when he died about 25 years ago, they played 'Wind Beneath My Wings' at his funeral. Every single time that song is on—usually at the supermarket or shopping mall—I'm in tears within seconds. Any song from *The Lion King* puts me in a good mood, as I took my parents to see the stage show while I was living in New York, a very happy memory for me.

Growing up, our house was full of music; a traditional old record player was the featured piece of furniture in our living room. The lid was permanently up and there was always vinyl spinning out the dulcet tones of an old-time crooner. Each week I would walk home from Sunday school with my sister, and as we turned the corner into our street we would hear the music playing (and smell Mum's roast in the oven—another big memory stimulant for me). Bing Crosby was a favourite, as was Dean Martin—and then heading towards the 1970s, Engelbert Humperdinck was on high rotation. When my parents discovered CDs, Michael Crawford became a particular favourite; sadly, that also meant that the UK sitcom *Some Mother's Do 'Ave 'Em* became must-watch TV.

Then came the André Rieu era. Without a word of a lie, every single time I visited my parents during their last three years in the family home, one of his DVDs was screening on the TV. I'm convinced there is some kind of hypnotic incantation hidden within his music that is addictive to anyone over the age of 65. Whatever it was, it had a calming and positive effect on my mother. She would sit for hours and watch those DVDs—they were kind of like a babysitter for her. When André Rieu was flexing his bow and prancing around that stage, Mum was not pacing, nor was she fidgeting or crying—she was tapping away with a huge smile on her face. So, André Rieu it was, and as often as we could.

Once Mum was in the nursing home, Dad relocated their entire CD collection to Mum's room, and he took it upon himself to ensure there was always music playing in the communal living area. He was spinning those discs like Fatboy

Slim, and god help anyone who tried to mess with his music. (My son grew up knowing the words to old folk songs, and instead of running around singing a Wiggles hit, would belt out 'Danny Boy'.) There was often a concert scheduled on the third floor, so Dad would wheel Mum up there for the show. He was from a generation that always arrived at least an hour early to ensure a good parking spot, or a good seat at the movies, or first dibs at the buffet, so Mum usually ended up in the front row. Now Mum at that time couldn't walk, talk or feed herself, but there seemed to be nothing wrong with her hearing, as she would often jump at the sound of a loud noise. Still, Dad would repeatedly position Mum up the front, right next to the speaker, and ten minutes into each performance he would have to wheel her away, as she was visibly unsettled by the noise. But sure enough, each week he would do the same thing. (I think the triumph of securing that position overtook his general commonsense. It's that mentality of taking what is on offer, even if it's something you are not remotely interested in—if it's free, or you're going to be first in line, then go for it. I often have to stop Dad stuffing his pockets full of bread rolls at the local pub because they are free at the buffet. He is so proficient at procuring anything that isn't nailed down that he will often unpack his bag at my house and reveal a stash of anything from napkins to sugar sachets, mini jam jars, single-serve butters—you name it.)

So, each time he would position Mum in the front row of these concerts, he would tell me about it that night during our phone call—about how there was a concert on, but it was 'way too loud for your mother' so he had to take her away. I would ask where they were sitting, and he would always say, 'We had a great seat right up the front.'

Sigh!

My cousin once took her mum (my mother's sister) to a Christmas concert in her nursing home. It was a very festive occasion, the room was appropriately decorated and the Christmas cheer was being spread around like gastro. My aunt and cousin were sitting towards the front (must run in the family), and throughout the one-hour concert they all sang along, having a gay old time. The final rendition of 'We Wish You a Merry Christmas' had just finished and everyone was cheering and clapping. The performer took a bow and stepped up to the microphone to thank the adoring audience.

'Thank you all very much! We hope you have a wonderful Christmas, and look forward to seeing you all here again next year.'

Pause.

'I bloody hope not!'

Yep, that was my auntie. We're not sure whether she didn't want that particular singer back next year, or whether she didn't want to still be in the nursing home the following Christmas, but either way, she felt pretty strongly about one of them. Tough gig for that guy.

The performances at Mum's nursing home weren't always musical. One afternoon a stand-up comedian had been booked to do a show. I wonder if he entertained the idea of cracking the same joke several times just to see if he could get away with it, but no—he had quite a routine planned out. He started off with the standard run-of-the-mill ageing jokes, of the 'You know you're old when . . .' variety. He was killing them (not literally). Had them rolling in the aisles (some literally).

One of his jokes even made it into Dad's repertoire: Did you hear the one about the elderly couple driving down the freeway and they hear a news alert on the radio to take care because there is a car driving the wrong way down the very freeway they were on? The driver turns to his wife and says, 'It's not just *one* car, honey, it's *hundreds* of them.'

Funny stuff, right? The comedian even rolled out the old classic, 'The best thing about Alzheimer's is that you can hide your own Easter eggs.'

And my personal favourite: The doctor asks his elderly patient if he is urinating and opening his bowels regularly. 'Of course,' the old man replies. 'Every morning I urinate at 7 a.m. and open my bowels around 8 a.m. Then at 9 a.m sharp I wake up.' Boom boom.

So, all was going well, until the end of his twenty-minute routine, when he ventured down the funeral-joke path. Dad said the room fell silent—that could also be because he has been virtually deaf for a while and refuses to wear his hearing aids. A funeral home is the next stop on the road of life for these fine folks, so funerals are not something they generally find hilarious, especially when they lose another resident from within the nursing home. I'm pretty sure 'can't-read-a-room comedian guy' didn't get called back for another gig, but he did give Dad quite a funny five-minute routine to bust out at family gatherings.

·

With dementia and Alzheimer patients, music is widely used in therapy, often as a form of communication and expression. Over the past decade, several studies and documentaries have shown how a familiar old song can unlock a seemingly dormant memory in the brain. And that although the brain of these patients may not be able to verbalise emotions or convey them physically, it can retain their ability to move in time with a beat, even late into the disease.

One remarkable video I have seen on YouTube is of a woman named Naomi Feil, who has developed a technique proving to be rather successful in connecting with dementia patients called 'validation therapy'. In this particular clip, Naomi is working with an elderly woman who, after being non-verbal for many years, starts to sing along with a song she remembers from her church-going days. Naomi starts by gently stroking the woman's face, which is meant to stim-ulate memories of how we were touched by our mothers as babies, and then she begins to softly sing to her. The patient soon begins to tap along with the music—but nearly five minutes into the clip, that particular song obviously unlocks a very significant memory in her brain, and this previously non-verbal patient starts to sing along with Naomi. Not a dry eye in the house.

After I first saw that clip, I was convinced that if we could find the right song and sing it to Mum, something in her brain would recognise it—and maybe, just maybe, we could, even for a fleeting moment, bring her back from where she was. It was worth a shot, so I thought a lot about what would be the perfect song. She loved all those old crooner tunes from Frank Sinatra and Dean Martin, and couldn't go past a good old-fashioned show tune in her day. Judy Garland's 'Somewhere Over the Rainbow' was her all-time favourite, but I knew I wouldn't get through one verse of that song without turning into a blubbering mess. It had to be something that brought her joy, but didn't take her back to a sad or emotional place.

I had it: the Collingwood Football Club theme song! She had supported that AFL team her whole life, and on the Saturdays we didn't all take the train to their home football ground and watch them play, Mum would be parked in the kitchen all day, cooking and listening to the game on the radio. That song was sung as the team ran onto the ground and then, god willing, after the game as part of the victory celebration. It was a perfect choice—and thankfully, you don't need to be Julie Andrews to sound half decent singing it. If 90,000 drunk football fans can sing it in public, then surely I can pull it off in front of my mother without causing too much embarrassment.

So off we went on the habitual Sunday morning visit. I had warned my husband there was a pretty good chance he was going to witness some kind of a miracle that morning; I'm surprised the thought of inviting a news crew along to record the action hadn't crossed my mind. After preparing myself emotionally, I stood in front of Mum, who was sleeping happily in her chair. I leant forward and slowly started to stroke her face, just like the woman in the video clip. Then I started singing softly in her ear. I got through the first verse and chorus, then stepped back to witness the awakening.

Nothing. She was still sleeping.

I leant in and repeated the process. Still nothing.

I did it a third time. More nothing.

At this point my husband went back to reading his paper. I mumbled something about her being very tired, then retreated to my seat to ponder why my singing therapy hadn't elicited even the slightest of responses.

After a few minutes I tried again. Still nothing.

I then decided to expand my repertoire. I tried a bit of 'New York, New York', followed by 'Quando, Quando, Quando' and then 'What's New Pussycat?'. I finally resorted to 'Somewhere Over the Rainbow'. Yep, I had played the trump card, at the risk of it being too emotional, and still nothing. Not one tear. Not even a twitch. She didn't open her eyes for that entire visit—quite possibly out of protest to my singing voice.

For the next few days I tried to make sense of why my singing therapy hadn't worked. Maybe it was too late—maybe

I should have started the awakening process earlier? Maybe it was just about trying different songs, until the right one hit?

It is amazing how, after losing a loved one to this disease, you spend quite a bit of time beating yourself up about what you could have done differently, to either prevent the disease (impossible), or slow it down (unlikely). After Mum was diagnosed we tried many things to keep her brain active, and I still think about what more we could have done. One of the problems is that the disease can involve such a slow decline, and symptoms such as being a bit forgetful are simply seen as a natural part of getting older, rather than reflecting an underlying disease. As mentioned earlier, I just figured Mum's brain had forgotten how to function fully because Dad had started doing everything for her.

If you suspect a loved one—or you yourself—may be suffering from the disease, there is so much advice and information available through Alzheimer's organisations to help guide you in the right direction. If nothing else, you will feel better about knowing you did what you could—but trust me, there will be days where you will feel you could have done more.

Many, many days.

16

To be brutally honest

Have you ever wondered why older people seem grumpy? I do. My father, at the age of 86, is very grumpy—my son is too loud, there is nothing on the television worth watching, things are too expensive now, the younger generation have no respect for the older, kids should be outside playing, not inside on their iPads.

Hang on. All of that is actually true! So maybe old people aren't grumpier, just more honest. Maybe at some point they just decide, to hell with it—I'm going to say what I think. And the older they get, the more honest they get.

There was a woman in Mum's nursing home who would constantly call out that she was choking. We would hear her all through the corridors—sometimes for an hour at a time. The first time I heard it I reacted as most visitors do, and ran to get a nurse. The nurse looked up from what she was doing and calmly told me not to panic, as this particular lady was in no actual danger of choking and it was just a ploy for attention. Even though for the most part I believed her, I couldn't really put out of my mind this idea that there was a woman screaming and choking in her room, so I decided to look in on her, just to reassure myself she really was okay. Her room was two doors up from the communal area, so I wandered up and leant partway in. She was calmly sitting up in a chair, knitting. She looked up as I entered the room and smiled at me, then went back to her knitting and yelling.

Knit one, pearl one, choke one, yell one.

She had quite the routine going. I can imagine how hearing it every day with some frequency might get on everyone's nerves.

One afternoon I was sitting in the communal area with Mum and Dad and we heard the first of the 'I'm choking!' calls ring out. Dad gave me that 'here we go again' look with a roll of his eyes. The next thing I knew, a resident wheeled her push walker past us with some level of urgency, mumbling to herself. Following her out of curiosity, I saw her stop at the door of The Choker. She lifted up her walker so it was just off the ground, then started banging it into the open door of the room. The Choker looked up at the commotion at her door; the agitated woman set her walker down and screamed, 'I hope you choke and then we won't have to hear you anymore!' Wow, that was quite the heckle—and probably echoed the sentiments of many in the facility. The disgruntled resident turned around and headed back towards me; I was now standing in the middle of the corridor like a stunned mullet. As she came level with me, she smiled and said, 'That will shut her up.' Off she wheeled with a sense of victory. I watched until she turned the corner, then went and sat back down with Dad. One minute later we heard 'I'm choking!' from the room two doors up.

You may notice when visiting nursing homes that most rooms have cute little signs on the doors displaying the resident's name, and usually a photo of them or a drawing from a grandchild (or artistically challenged loved one). On Mum's door we had a nice picture of her, with her name. Nothing too flash—just whose room this is, and this is her name. Maybe the real purpose of these door signs is to help residents remember which room was theirs? One woman decided it was her job to move these signs around. As if these people aren't confused enough: you leave your room for a cup of tea as a lovely-looking older lady named Betty only to return ten minutes later and discover you are now a 90-year-old man with a Greek fishing cap who goes by the name of George.

My husband's grandmother lived to the age of 98, and was as honest as they came. A woman in her nursing home named Wendy, who resided on the same floor, also had her name and photo on the door, which showed a largish woman with grey curly hair and a big cheerful smile; underneath the photo was her nickname, 'Grandma Hugs'. One afternoon, my husband remarked to his grandma that 'Grandma Hugs' seemed like a nice lady. Grandma looked up from the TV—whose company she clearly preferred to ours—and said, 'If she tries to hug *me* I will push her to the ground!' She would've been lucky to tip the scales at around 40 kilos, whereas Grandma Hugs weighed in at around 90 kilos. In her case at least, it seems brutal honesty was a source of strength that could overcome any physical shortcomings.

Another time we were sitting in her room at the nursing home as my mother-in-law was sorting through some clothes in a chest at the foot of her bed that Grandma had decided were to be thrown out. Each piece of clothing was brought out and held up for Grandma to assess and perhaps salvage. A lovely cream-coloured cardigan with pastel hand-knitted flowers sewn onto the lapels was offered up. Casting her eyes upon the garment, she threw her arms up and declared, 'Get rid of it, it's awful.' My mother-in-law took a breath and awkwardly explained that she'd bought that cardigan only a few months ago and Grandma had seemed to like it. Grandma asked for a closer inspection of the cardigan, ran her fingers across the flowers and said, 'Well, I didn't care for it then, and I don't care for it now.' Yep, that's honesty for you.

Then of course there's that fine line between honesty and Alzheimer's. One example of that was when my normal-sized and nicely groomed cousin walked into her mum's nursing home one afternoon with a beautiful bunch of flowers. It wasn't Mother's Day, or her mother's birthday—it was just a simple gesture to say I love you and I hope these flowers brighten up your day. She got no more than five steps inside her mum's room and my aunt said, 'If you put on any more weight your arse won't fit through that door! And what have you done to your hair? You look a hundred.' You can only hope that the flowers all drooped and a downbeat kind of 'bup bow' comedy sound effect filled the room. What makes a mother say that to her daughter?

Clearly someone who has Alzheimer's or dementia can't really control their emotions, and in turn what they end up saying to people, so there is no point being offended in these situations. Mum never went down that brutally honest path. She was virtually the opposite—always a wonderfully supportive and happy person. One of the last words I remember her saying with any regularity was 'beautiful'. She used it in reference to everything.

'How is that meal, Mum?'

'Beautiful.'

'Are you feeling okay today, Mum?'

'Beautiful.'

'Do you need to go to the toilet, Mum?'

'Beautiful.'

We were thankful Mum had latched onto such a lovely, positive word. One gentleman in her facility had only two words in his vocabulary: 'piss' and 'off'. Used together in succession. About everything, and to everyone. Even my young son. (It's amazing how toddlers store things in their tiny little minds and then recall them at the most inopportune time.)

One place in nursing homes where honesty is in full flight is the dining room. Of course, nobody expects a five-star meal in these facilities—and with a fair number of the meals vitamised, it seems pointless to cook up a beautiful piece of marbled wagu and then pulse it in the blender. So it's cereal, toast and fruit for breakfast, casserole or cold cuts and salad for lunch, then pasta or roast for dinner. I have to admit there were days I couldn't quite determine the specific type of meat on offer, but it was definitely a protein, I think. What I do know is that the meals are planned around dietary and nutritional requirements, and served up to 100 people in each sitting, and to a budget, so there are times when the food is going to be a little less than hot, and a little less appetising than something prepared by Heston Blumenthal.

Dad knew this, and I knew he knew it, but he would continually complain about the food. Every night I would get the rundown of the three meals and how it was beyond him that anyone could serve that food up to human beings. How he had taken her lunch plate back to the server and complained it was cold, or the meat was tough, or the vegies weren't cooked enough. One time he even took a piece of rockmelon back to the kitchen because it was a bit green. To be fair, Dad wasn't the only one complaining about the food—but instead of walking their plates back to the kitchen, or asking one of the staff if they could have their apple pie reheated, some residents would throw the food. Throw it on the ground, throw it at the carers, throw it at each other.

Throughout the dining room you could hear the reviews of the meal, accompanied by expletives as a bowl of custard hit the dirt. An elderly man who often sat at Mum's table needed to be fed by a carer, who would load up a spoon full of vitamised goodness and lift it towards his mouth, just as his arm would slap it away, sending the food and utensil flying through the air like some kind of tasty missile.

Another resident had her own personal form of protest. She would take her teeth out at the dining table and set them on the plate next to her food and refuse to put them back in until the food was prepared to her satisfaction. I bet the other residents fought over who got to sit at her table every day. Nothing spikes the appetite more than a nice set of false teeth sitting on the table—yummo, pass the salt please.

Mum, though, was a good eater, probably because Dad made it his mission to force every piece of food into her mouth, whether she was hungry or not. I think my mother was the only woman who, after a couple of years residing in the nursing home, had put on ten kilos. While everyone else was complaining about the food, the response I got from Mum, every time I asked her how lunch or dinner was, was always the same: 'Beautiful.'

17

All aboard

Sitting in a nursing home all day can become quite monotonous for residents. If they are not confined to wheelchairs, there is at least lots of room to wander around, in an environment that is always safe. But it is nice to have an outing—so when the minibus pulls up outside it is an occasion for much joy and excitement.

These outings are planned weeks in advance, with a certain level of forethought as to where to go, and the best combination of residents to take. At Mum's facility there was usually only room for one wheelchair on the bus, and if Mum didn't get that spot, Dad was not a happy camper. He'd get a sniff of any upcoming outing and would march straight to the manager's office to make sure Mum's name was on that list. It usually worked out okay, because if they took Mum, they also got the added bonus of Dad, who could in effect act as another helper. Trips to nurseries and outdoor cafes seemed to be the best locations, as they give the residents a bit of room to move around.

Much as Dad enjoyed taking Mum out on the bus, there was always a downside: there was always a 'chucker'. Yep, a seat on the 'vomit comet' wasn't always the best place to be on a warm summer's day. Dad has a pretty strong stomach, but if the vomit happened early-ish in the journey, the smell was pretty intense by the time they arrived at their location, and put a bit of a downer on the whole trip.

Me, I do not have a strong stomach at all. I am what is known as a 'sympathetic vomiter'. If someone vomits within a ten-metre radius of me, up it comes. As a child I shared a room with my sister, and if she got sick during the night, Mum would grab a bucket for my sister, and then Dad would have to grab one for me. My friends in high school would go into the toilet cubicle next to me and pretend to vomit by half flushing the toilet (pretty accurate sound effect) until they got me started. Another time, at my cousin's twenty-first birthday party, Mum said she wasn't feeling well, and before you knew it I was outside the local footy club hosing down shoes. We had driven Mum and Dad to the party, and on the drive home I had my window down and my head hanging out like a labrador on a summer's day.

So if the nursing home minibus made it to the destination free of incident, then it was usually a nice outing for the residents. The hardest part was keeping them all together once you got there—like herding cats. I often see lines of kindergarten children walking down the street with rope or ribbon tied around their waists to keep them walking in line together—but I guess you can't do that with the elderly (especially if The Choker was in the group, and somebody else was actually choking—nobody would pay any attention). So it's all about keeping everyone together and staying vigilant.

Outings were also a big-ticket item at my aunt's nursing home. One particular day they headed off to the local RSL, and my aunt was first on the bus—she loved a bit of a play on the pokies, and had been looking forward to it for days. Clearly it was never the intention to take a group of Alzheimer patients out to gamble, so when they arrived, they were ushered into a room set up with a long table and chairs, well away from the gaming area—much to the dismay of my aunt, who had so many gold coins in her handbag it was a wonder she could lift it. After initially sitting down with the other residents for a cup of tea and pre-lunch nibble, she started getting itchy feet, and when the carers weren't looking, made her way to the gaming room. Within a minute or two she was apprehended and escorted back into their lunch area. But five minutes later, she had slipped through the cracks again. After her second attempt, they stationed an RSL staff member at the entrance of the gaming room to stop any further endeavours. Even so, she managed to break out again—but instead of heading to the gaming room, she left the building and hailed a cab down the road. Imagine the surprise on my cousin's face when her mum turned up on her doorstep ranting and raving about how she'd been denied her right to gamble. (It's those kind of stories that illustrate how instinct can kick in: my aunt couldn't tell you what she did that morning, but had enough wits and long-term memory working for her that she could hail a cab and give the driver her daughter's address.)

One afternoon, my cousin took her for an X-ray of her thumb. There were no parking spots outside the radiology rooms, so she dropped her mum at the entrance and asked her to wait there while she parked. A few minutes later, when she arrived at the front door, her mum was nowhere to be found. No sign of her in the car park, so she ventured inside for a look. Not in the waiting room. My cousin asked the receptionist, who indifferently shook her head. Investigating further, my cousin found my my aunt meandering around the CT area. Fugitive back in custody, they managed to get the X-ray done. My cousin then asked reception if they could watch her mum while she fetched the car, and was pleasantly surprised to see her mum sitting patiently in the reception area when she pulled up out the front. She loaded her mum into the car, but just as they were about to drive off, my aunt said she was missing her handbag. A quick check of the back seat; no sign of the handbag. My cousin turned the car off, took the keys with her (her mum had never driven a car, but today could be the day she decided to start!) and found the handbag sitting under a chair in the reception area. Back in the car park, she jumped in the car, only to find the passenger seat empty. She looked around the car park just in time to see her mum marching towards the main road at a cracking pace. When she'd caught up, my anxious cousin scolded her mum for not waiting in the car; my aunt retorted that she was simply going to the bus stop, as she had clearly been left behind and nobody was going to drive her home.

We were quite lucky that Mum never managed to success-fully wander off on us. As her conditioned worsened, while they were still living at home, Dad tried to get her out on little trips as often as he could—drives around her childhood neighbourhood, trips to the local shops for a coffee and sand-wich. They would visit our house a few times a week so Dad could just potter in our garden, knowing Mum was safe inside with me. But these trips were not easily executed. Trying to get Mum in a car was like the ancient and intricate art of origami. If you didn't do each step in the right order, you had no hope. Not only could she not comprehend what we were asking her to do, but her limbs would stiffen, making it almost impossible to get her into the right position so we could lift her into the passenger seat. We would get her arms in the right configuration, but once we moved on to the legs, the arms would straighten again—like trying to fold the bottom of a cardboard box into that formation where you theoretically don't need to tape it up. I always use tape—but I couldn't really use tape on Mum.

Nursing homes generally do a great job of fostering activities to help stimulate those residents who can't actually go out for day trips. Dad's garden club is still a regular fixture on the weekly in-house social and leisure calendar at Mum's old nursing home. Another popular fixture is bingo. Now there's an interesting concept: who thought it'd be a good idea to sit a bunch of dementia patients down with bingo cards and call out numbers, expecting them to fill out their cards correctly? The bingo sessions I witnessed were like walking into a toy store and setting off all the talking animals. The bingo caller would get through maybe three balls and someone would call out 'Bingo!'—that would start a chain reaction, with the calls of 'Bingo!' coming thick and fast. Clearly nobody could actually have bingo after three balls, so the caller would continue calling to around the six-ball mark. She would then get up and wander around to every patient who was holding up a card and was shouting out 'Bingo!' over and over again—which was most of them—and then, after ascertaining that none of them was a winner, she would resume her chair, call out the next number, and the process would continue for the next half hour. One afternoon while we were sitting with Mum, my brother heard a bingo game start up in the communal living room. He thought it would be funny to call out 'Bingo!' to see if it would set off a chain reaction. It did. (Remember, he is also the kind of guy who tells his younger sister she was adopted.)

Another favourite event on the social calendar is fancy dress day. I realise it's fun for residents to dress up and have a party—but aren't they confused enough? To be sitting opposite Superman for afternoon tea might be a little confronting for someone who wears their underwear over their trousers for all the wrong reasons. Look to your right and hello, you're sitting next to Pocahontas. And there goes the Easter bunny . . . in September? Perhaps they should also have a 'Dress In Your Normal Clothes, Put On The Correct Way' day. No misbuttoned cardigans. No odd shoes, or shirts on inside out. And definitely no naked strolls around the corridors.

The monthly newsletters in the communal areas keep the residents and their families updated on all the latest and upcoming events, including celebrations, residents' birthdays, anniversaries and the like. One particular event caught my eye:

Wednesday, 9 May—Girls With Gadgets will be doing a presentation in the 3rd floor dining room. Gentlemen, you are more than welcome to come along and see the demonstration. I'm sure there will be gadgets that you will find useful. More details on the noticeboard.

The dictionary tells us that a gadget is an 'ingenious device'. If these girls were trying to bring something ingenious into the lives of these dementia patients, I think they might have been in for a tough sell, as most of these patients can't even feed themselves. Still, I'm guessing they pulled a capacity crowd that afternoon.

Craft days are another highlight on the calendar. It's always good to have some kind of activity that keeps residents stimulated, and craft absolutely ticks that box. It was amazing to see how clever and skilled they could be when they were doing something that was obviously still ingrained from years of practice. Tables would be strewn with ribbons and polystyrene balls, string, glue and paper—and all the wonderful knick-knacks created during these craft sessions would be sold at the annual Christmas stall. In a spirit of democracy, Dad bought one of everything that anyone had made—his unit in the week before Christmas could've featured in a television episode of *Hoarders: Christmas Spirit*. He'd buy enough tree decorations, Christmas card holders, tissue box holders and doilies to cater for the dining room at Hogwarts.

These crafty creations would also adorn every door handle within the nursing home, and Christmas spirit was always in abundance. There were always the most magnificently decorated Christmas trees on every level—or should I say, the Christmas trees started out magnificently decorated, but after a couple of weeks would all be looking a little worse for wear.

One lady on Mum's floor, Dot, took quite a fancy to the decorations on the communal tree; she would spend much of her time trying to pluck them off and spirit them back to her room. She wasn't a tall woman, so her procuring was limited to the lower limbs of the tree. Her style was not to get an armful and stagger back to her room and unload the lot; instead, she would just gradually pick away—maybe part of her knew that nobody would notice one or two missing each morning and afternoon. The carers would find them tucked away on a shelf in her cupboard, and would just put them back on the tree at the end of each week. It was like a well-rehearsed dance of kleptomania where nobody ends up in jail. No real harm done, and we found it quite entertaining to see if we could catch Dot in the act.

One morning, a little glint of Christmas sitting high on the tree caught Dot's attention. Nothing was going to stop her getting her hands on that tinselled gem. She started off by pulling some of the lower branches down, to bend the top of the tree down towards her, but as she let go of a branch with one hand to grab another, the limb would flip back up and almost take her out with it. Then she started jumping up to reach the decoration, but given the shape of a Christmas tree, that was always going to end badly. You can't jump up without jumping in—which is precisely what she did. All we heard was a crash, a thud, and the sound of breaking glass.

Everyone jumped up and ran to the tree. It was lying on its side, with the lights still flashing, and baubles rolling away at a rapid rate. Dot was nowhere to be seen, so we all assumed she had claimed her prize and left the scene of the crime. Then, in weirdly similar fashion to the scene from *The Wizard of Oz* where those ruby slippers can be seen under Dorothy's house, we noticed a Grosby slipper poking out from a lower limb. The tree had fallen on top of Dot, and she was pinned beneath it. Luckily the tree was an artificial one and didn't weigh a ton, so we managed to lift it up and get Dot to her feet; she hadn't suffered any ill effects from her efforts. The broken remnants were safely cleared away, and all the wayward decorations rounded up. Well, almost all the decorations were recovered—Dot had managed to knock her prize bauble off the top of the tree and had her spindly little fingers tightly wrapped around it. She deserved that decoration. I hope it remains in her family, passed down from generation to generation as a treasured possession.

Christmas decorations were not the only objects of Dot's desire. She was also quite fond of a man in uniform. So much so that every couple of weeks Dot would activate the fire alarm at the nursing home, just so the fire brigade would show up. Dad said she loved seeing those lovely red fire engines show up, all shiny and big—but part of me thinks she quite liked seeing those brave firemen show up, all shiny and big. I was there one afternoon when Dot got a hankering for a firey, and although the staff were always pretty sure the alarm was just triggered by Dot pushing the button, they of course needed to take the alarm seriously and thoroughly check the building. The fire station was just down the road, so the big red engine would arrive before anyone could call in the false alarm. The sound of the sirens pulling into the car park always created a frenzied dash to the balconies for a front-row view of the drama not about to unfold. In some way I got the sense that if it was a quiet day at the fire station, the firemen would all take a drive just for something to do. An outing for them, and at least an hour's worth of entertainment for the nursing home—wins all round.

My aunt's nursing home also had regular smoke alarm incidents. First they would hear a loud beeping sound, and then quite often the sprinklers would activate. So where there is smoke there is fire, right? Not always. Turned out that where there was smoke, there was a smoker. One particular gentlemen resident would somehow manage to get cigarettes smuggled into the nursing home, on a worryingly regular basis, and every now and then would set off the alarm. Old Mr Marlboro man just loved to smoke. It wasn't as if he hid his addiction to tobacco. If anyone visited the home, he would wander up behind them, appearing almost out of nowhere, and in a deep, whispery voice enquire, 'Got a smoke?' I just hope he wasn't sneaking into other residents' rooms in the middle of the night, leaning over their bed, waiting for their eyes to open, and asking, 'Got a smoke?'

Maybe he worked on the theory that if he asked often enough, and asked enough people, someone at some point would actually give him a cigarette—perhaps another resident's family members feeling sorry for him, or maybe a carer who got tired of him asking, or maybe members of his own family who were trying to make him happy in the only way they knew how.

Maybe, every time he asked, they should say he'd just had one—after all, he *did* have Alzheimer's.

18

Pushed to the limit

Once Mum was in the nursing home and became less and less mobile, we thought it was time to buy her a wheelchair of her own, rather than use one of the empty ones lying around the facility, of which about three were up for grabs at any given time on any given day—especially when we came across one that hadn't been cleaned down properly after the last resident had vacated it, sending my germ-a-phobe tendencies into overdrive.

First I thought about looking on eBay, but felt a bit nervous about getting one in less than perfect working condition, and then began freaking about why someone would be selling a perfectly good wheelchair—what happened to the person who was using it, and why don't they need it anymore? My mind went into crazy-person mode and I closed the eBay window.

Plan B. I did a general Google search for wheelchairs and found quite a few suppliers in our area. To save myself some groundwork, I decided to simply ring to see what they had in stock, and maybe just buy one over the phone—easy peasy, all sorted, job well done.

Not so much. The first company put me through to a salesman to outline all the options. I explained that the wheelchair was for my mother to use for outings, so we just wanted something comfortable and lightweight that we could simply throw in the car, yadda yadda yadda. Then the questions started.

'Will you be needing attendant handbrakes?'

'Umm, not entirely sure what that even is.'

'Will your mother be operating the wheelchair herself, or will an attendant be pushing her?'

'My father will be pushing her.'

'Well then, you'll be needing attendant handbrakes.'

'Okay then.'

'Are you after a steel frame, or aluminium frame?'

'What's the difference?'

'One is made out of steel, and one is made out of aluminium.'

This was clearly not going well.

Salesman: 'How much does your mother weigh?'

'Not sure, exactly . . .'

'Do you know how tall she is?'

'Won't she be sitting down?'

'Maybe it's best that you just come to a showroom and we can look at suitable models.'

'Okay then'. I think I may have underestimated this.

So off I went, down to the wheelchair showroom, with a bit more research under my belt—including my mum's height and weight.

Riding in a wheelchair and using a cash register—they were the two things that fascinated me as a kid, and I'd always had a yearning to try both. I worked as a checkout chick in my late teens, so managed to tick the cash register box early on, but had never actually sat in a wheelchair. Of course I know that being confined to one isn't a barrel of laughs, but I'd always thought it would be rather fun whizzing around on four wheels, if just for a minute.

I wandered around the showroom, waiting for the right moment. As the only salesperson on the floor disappeared through double doors, my door of opportunity swung open. I lowered myself into a speedy-looking model, keen for a quick spin. The seat was comfy, my feet were placed perfectly on the little footrests, my hands ready on the wheel hoops, and off I went. I rolled forwards a little, then tried to turn left, but got my fingers caught in the wheel hoop and jammed my foot into the model parked next to me. I backed that baby up and tried again, this time pulling out unscathed, and started up the aisle at a snail's pace, in a kind of zig-zaggy way. It's not as easy as it looks, and by the end of the aisle my arms were exhausted. Let's just say I developed a new-found respect for people who manage to get themselves from point A to point B in a wheelchair.

Then from behind me a voice asked, 'Can I help you?' Ahh, the old 'Second Salesperson on the Showroom Floor' trick, hey? That was my cue to get out of the wheelchair, but with those footrests, there is no graceful way of doing it. I just kind of stumbled forward, sending the wheelchair backwards, straight into the legs of the salesperson behind me.

Off to a good start then.

I explained I was after a wheelchair for my mother—one with a modular, lightweight aluminium frame and attendant brakes. I was very proud of my new knowledge of wheelchairs, until the questions started coming thick and fast again.

Do you need swing-away, flip-up and/or removable footrests? Do you need swing-away armrests? Solid tyres or pneumatic wheels? Anti-tip bars? Adjustable castors, wheel hoops? Rear wheel locks? Quick-release rear wheels? Seat width, seat length, seat height? Backrest height, backrest angle? Front seat length, front seat height? Footrest length, footplate angle? Storage pocket?

Ahh, I know what a storage pocket is, and one of those would be handy. As for everything else above . . . um, I think so?

Over an hour later, we had an appropriate model selected. But wait, there's more.

What kind of accessories do you want? Standard cushion, air cushion, pressure-distribution cushion, contoured cushion, comfort heat and moisture-distribution cushion? Do you want a cushion with smart cells? What about sheepskin covers for the seat cushion and arm rests?

Holy smokes, Batman! I just want Mum to sit in a wheel-chair and be comfortable. Is that too much to ask?

'And what colour were you thinking—and do you want a powder-coat finish, or a gloss paint?'

Kill me now, please.

So I walked out 90 minutes later with a brand-spanking-new red, lightweight wheelchair with solid tyres, removable footrests, padded armrests, contoured cushion and attendant brakes. With a storage pocket. Woo hoo! As I drove home with that bad boy loaded into my hatchback, I couldn't help looking in my rear-vision mirror and admiring my new purchase — folded up and slightly obscuring my view through the back of the car.

The idea was to give it to Mum for Christmas as a present from us three kids, so I thought it might be nice to buy a big red bow to put on it, as wrapping it could prove even trickier than actually buying it. This was the week before Christmas, so I did have a bit of shopping to do after I left the 'Nuthin' but Wheelchairs' shop. As I drove around my local shopping centre, parking spots were proving a little elusive. Up and down the car park aisles I drove, feeling the Christmas spirit slowly draining with every horn tooted and the screech of every wheel. I spied an empty spot, started to pull into it, then realised it was a disabled parking space.

As I reversed back out, a glint of shiny red paint caught my eye. I sat for a good five minutes looking at that parking spot, looking at my new purchase in the rear-vision mirror, looking at that parking spot, looking in the rear-vision mirror. The wheelchair was in full view of everyone, so if I *did* park there nobody would bat an eyelid. How would it be any different to those mums who keep prams in their cars years after their children have outgrown them, just so they can park in the 'parking with prams' spots? And I was only going to run in and grab a ribbon—and maybe a few other items, seeing as I found such a good parking spot. Sure, I wasn't disabled, and didn't have a disabled sticker on my car, but I *did* have a wheelchair crammed into my hatchback in full view . . .

Finally honesty prevailed, and I slowly joined the line of waiting cars, tooting and screeching my way around that car park. Bah, humbug!

19

Signs—sealed and delivered

It seemed like the longest time that Mum was just existing comfortably in her own little world in the nursing home. One of the hardest things about having a loved one with Alzheimer's is that the disease affects everyone differently, and its progression, in terms of a time line, can be difficult to predict.

I kept waiting for obvious signs of decline—major issues that would indicate where she was at in terms of the disease, but nothing really happened. I did some research into the different stages of Alzheimer's, looking for some kind of reliable guide to tell me what to expect and when, so I could be fully equipped with it. Every time Dad threw something new about Mum's behaviour into a conversation I would Google for hours to see if it was a significant signpost of the disease.

Most research charts the progression of Alzheimer's disease using either a three-stage model, or a seven-stage one.

THREE-STAGE MODEL

For those who like their information condensed, this is the three-stage disease model.

Stage one: Mild/early

The first stage can last anywhere from two to four years. There is frequent memory loss, particularly of recent conversations and events. The person may ask repeated questions, and may have some problems expressing and understanding language. They may need reminders for daily activities, and have mild coordination problems, making writing, driving and using objects difficult. Depression and apathy can occur, accompanied by mood swings.

Stage two: Moderate/middle

In the second stage, which can last between two and ten years, the signs become more apparent, and the person can no longer cover up their problems. There is pervasive and persistent memory loss, including of their own personal history, and the person may be unable to recognise friends and family. Their speech may be rambling, their reasoning unusual, and they may be confused about current events, what time it is, or where they are. They are more likely to become lost in familiar settings. Sleep disturbances or delusions are common, and the person may experience changes in mood and behaviour, such as aggression and uninhibited behaviour, which can be aggravated by stress and change. Mobility and coordination are affected by slowness, rigidity and tremors. The person needs structure and reminders, and assistance with activities of daily living.

Stage three: Severe/late

In this stage, which may last from one to three years or more, the person will need round-the-clock intensive support and care. They are generally incapacitated, with severe to total loss of verbal skills, and are unable to care for themselves. The person is confused about the past and present, and unable to remember, communicate, or process information. There may be problems with swallowing, incontinence and illness, and extreme problems with mood, behaviour, hallucinations and delirium. Falls are possible, and immobility likely.

SEVEN-STAGE MODEL

For those who like a bit more meat on their bones, here are the seven stages of Alzheimer's.

Stage one: No impairment

During this stage, Alzheimer's disease is not detectable and no memory problems or other symptoms of dementia are evident.

Stage two: Very mild decline/normal forgetfulness

The patient may notice minor memory problems or lose things around the house, although not to the point where the memory loss can easily be distinguished from normal age-related memory loss, as about half of all people over 65 begin noticing problems in concentration and word recall. The person will still do well on memory tests, and the disease is unlikely to be detected by physicians or loved ones.

Stage three: Mild decline/mild cognitive impairment

This stage can last from two to seven years. The person's friends and family may begin to notice memory and cognitive problems; the person may frequently lose personal possessions, including valuables. As the changes are subtle, the person may consciously or subconsciously try to cover up for their problems. A key feature is difficulty finding the right word during conversations, remembering names of new acquaintances, and difficulty planning and organising, which may affect life at home and work. Depression and other changes in mood may also occur. Physicians will be able to detect impaired cognitive function on memory and cognitive tests.

Stage four: Moderate decline/mild Alzheimer's

During this stage, which may last up to two years, clear-cut symptoms are apparent. Most people in this stage still know themselves and family members. They may have difficulty carrying out sequential tasks, including cooking, driving, ordering food at restaurants and shopping. They often withdraw from social situations and become defensive about their condition. They have difficulty with simple arithmetic, may forget details about their life history, have poor short-term memory (may not recall what they ate for breakfast, for example), and are unable to manage their finances and pay bills.

Stage five: Moderately severe decline/early dementia

The average duration of this stage is about eighteen months. During this stage, the decline is more severe. Patients start needing help with many daily activities such as eating and dressing appropriately. They experience a severe decline in numerical abilities and judgement skills, which can leave them vulnerable to safety issues. They may experience significant confusion, and be unable to recall simple details about themselves, such as their own phone number.

On the other hand, patients in stage five maintain a modicum of functionality. They often can still bathe and toilet independently. They also usually still know their family members and some detail about their personal history, especially their childhood and youth.

Stage six: Severe decline/middle dementia

The average duration of this stage is about two and a half years. Patients need constant supervision, and frequently require professional care. They lack an awareness of present events, may be confused about or unaware of their environment and surroundings, and cannot accurately remember the past, including most details of their personal history. The person is unable to recognise faces, except those of closest friends and relatives. They start to communicate pleasure and pain via behaviour; major personality changes are common. Agitation and hallucinations often present in the late afternoon or evening, and suspicion of family members is common. The person will need assistance with activities of daily living, such as toileting and bathing, due to loss of bowel and bladder control. Wandering is also common.

Stage seven: Very severe decline

The duration of this stage is impacted by the patient's quality of care, but the average length is one to two and a half years. Because Alzheimer's disease is a terminal illness, patients in stage seven are nearing death. They lose the ability to respond to their environment or communicate. They may still be able to utter words and phrases, but have no insight into their condition, and require total support for all functions of daily living. In the final stages, patients may lose their ability to swallow.

•

So, these were my guides to the progression of Mum's disease—although some of the stages in these two models seemed a bit nonsensical (and downright alarming) to me.

For instance, stage one of the first model, where no signs of Alzheimer's are present, would suggest we are *all* in stage one of Alzheimer's!

With the second model, one of the possible symptoms of stage four is 'an impaired ability to perform challenging mental arithmetic, for example, to count backwards from 75 by 7s'. Umm, that's me—really freaking out now.

And here's another symptom of stage four: 'decreased capacity to perform complex tasks, such as planning dinner for guests, paying bills and managing finances'. And there goes my husband!

You can see from those simple guidelines how hard it can be to accurately nail down what stage of Alzheimer's a person may actually be in, as well as a survival time line. Mum was still living in the family home right up to stage six of the second model, and then seemingly sat at stage seven for about six years.

I guess the reason I had such a morbid fascination with trying to lock down a time line was that we couldn't plan our future with Mum existing in this land of limbo. Every trip we tried to plan to visit my husband's family in the US was always reliant on Mum's health at the time—and even then I felt stressed about being so far away from her, and guilty for leaving Dad. My sister owns a travel agency and was overseas quite a bit, so we always tried to coordinate it so at least one of us would be in the country at any given time. I found it harder and harder to talk about events in the future, and became consumed by Mum's health and how much longer she would be around. We avoided talking about upcoming celebrations around Dad, as most of the time he wouldn't attend, and we didn't want him to feel left out.

While the symptoms of Alzheimer's disease clearly worsen over time, research shows that the rate of progression varies from patient to patient. On average a person with officially diagnosed Alzheimer's disease lives four to eight years after diagnosis—but can live for up to twenty years, depending on a wide range of factors. There is no way Mum would have survived the disease for thirteen years if it hadn't been for Dad's ongoing hands-on care.

For the most part, Mum had no major health issues in the nursing home, aside from the occasional cold and urinary tract infection, or UTI for short. UTIs are quite common in nursing homes, particularly in Alzheimer patients, and are often caused by poor hygiene, or the bladder not emptying completely. Many dementia and Alzheimer patients become incontinent and can sit for hours before their pads are changed, so these infections are sometimes hard to avoid—especially as they can't communicate, or convey their level of pain or discomfort; they sit and suffer in silence. And to make matters worse, one symptom of an advanced urinary tract infection is sudden confusion or delirium—but confusion is status quo with most dementia patients, so who is going to notice that Beryl on level two is acting strange? Lucky for us, Dad was devotedly on hand to notice any drastic changes in Mum's behaviour, so when she did succumb to a UTI—and she did have quite a few during her time there—these were treated in a timely manner.

Chest infections were another recurring health issue with Mum. These can take a more serious nature in Alzheimer patients in the later stages of the disease, if they have lost their ability to swallow adequately—but once again, Dad was always on the case, and any sign of a cough or gurgle was jumped on quick smart. The staff, too, were always very attentive with Mum—how could they not be, with Dad around?

.

One Thursday evening Dad arrived at our house for the traditional fish and chip sleepover. From his bag he produced a document that the nursing home manager had given him. It was a patient care information sheet; it was time to update Mum's records and ensure all her details were accurate, so we filled in all the boxes, just as we had every year before.

When we got to the end of the document, I discovered an additional page stapled at the back, which I hadn't seen before.

It was a DNR form.

A 'Do Not Resuscitate' form.

I know these forms are pretty commonplace when a loved one has been diagnosed with a terminal disease, and my rational side knew it was inevitable that we'd one day have to fill out one of these forms, but part of me still didn't want to acknowledge that Mum did indeed have a terminal illness.

A DNR is a medical directive issued by a doctor, at the request of a patient who is at the end of their life, or after consultation with the patient's next of kin or legal guardian. It basically instructs the medical staff within a hospital or care facility not to perform cardiopulmonary resuscitation (CPR) if the patient suffers a cardiac arrest, or if their breathing stops. Instead, the patient is left to die naturally, with measures taken to promote comfort during the dying process.

Pretty confronting stuff to be making decisions about. Mum was at some point going succumb to this horrible disease—but clearly, in the event of a heart attack, we would want her to still live, wouldn't we?

I read over this form in my head, trying to digest it all, especially the boxes where we needed to tick yes or no indicating whether to perform CPR.

Dad was reading over my shoulder and said, 'Just say, Do Not Resuscitate.'

Now, I knew that it was Dad's voice because a) I recognised it, and b) he was the only one in the room. But why would my father *not* want to have his wife of 55 years, who he clearly loved more than life itself, resuscitated? I turned around and looked at him, thinking he was a bit confused.

'You mean, *do* perform CPR,' I clarified.

'No—do not resuscitate,' he repeated.

At this point I was pretty sure he hadn't quite wrapped his head around all the terminology: too many letters in all of this DNR and CPR talk—obviously nothing was making sense to him.

'So you are saying that if Mum suffers a heart attack, you *don't* want her to be resuscitated?' I asked, getting genuinely concerned.

'Well,' he answered calmly, 'I don't think she would want to be resuscitated—do you?'

Well thanks very much for your input Dr Kevorkian, I felt like retorting, but stopped to think before I next spoke.

'So you mean to say that if your wife of 55 years—our mother—was lying on a table having suffered a heart attack, you would calmly stand by and say to the doctors, *Nup, don't bother, mate, let her go?*'

It came out a little harsher than I had intended, but I really wanted to be sure he understood the enormity of this decision—which legally was his decision to make.

He didn't answer, which made me realise he *had* actually thought about this, and maybe had decided Mum had suffered long enough. She *had* suffered long enough, but even though she wasn't showing any real signs of leaving us in the imme- diate future, I seriously couldn't imagine standing by and watching doctors do nothing if they had the ability to save her—and I couldn't for one minute imagine that, in that precise moment, Dad could either.

A friend of mine had a DNR issued by her family for her grandfather. Everyone had agreed on the decision with sound minds, as he was very old, frail and had been suffering for a long while; they felt it was the right thing to let him go when it was his time. When her grandfather's heart did give out, most of the family were at his bedside. The doctors came in with a CPR unit—then somebody announced he was a DNR and his wishes should be respected. At that moment, my friend's mother started yelling at the doctors to do everything they could to save him—she was desperate for her father not to pass on in that moment, even though she had agreed with the DNR decision when it was made the previous year. That scene in the hospital was very distressing for everyone, and to this day that family still has issues around it.

So I explained to Dad that if a time came when Mum was lying in a hospital having a cardiac arrest, I couldn't imagine we would all be happy to follow through with a DNR decision made months or even years before. In my mind, it would be easier for us to decide to let her go without the emotion of the moment confusing our decision. Bring in every doctor there is, every piece of equipment that beeps, to keep our mother alive, until we can decide as a united front that it was the right time to let her go. You can consent to a DNR on the spot, but it's harder to reverse one.

Dad agreed. He ticked the right box—or at least the one that felt right to me.

20

The circle of life

Christmases, birthdays, Mother's Days, Father's Days all came and went, and we fell into the routine of celebrating any family celebrations twice: once at the nursing home so Mum and Dad could be present, and then again at someone else's house so we could pretend that everything was normal. We never questioned the importance of spending time with Mum and Dad at the nursing home, but we never really left there thinking, 'Wow, Mum looks a little better today.' Once she got to the stage of basically being asleep each time we visited, we weren't spending quality time with her. It was a depressing decline, so slow it almost went unnoticed.

The day finally came when the nurse suggested Mum's food should be vitamised, as she was losing her ability to chew and swallow properly. This was one of those stages that I had read about, and was dreading. Not only could she choke if food sat in her throat, but she was succumbing to mouth ulcers and infections from keeping food in her mouth too long.

So the Sunday roast at the nursing home became the Sunday mash. The irony wasn't lost on me that for the past few years, my mother and my son were basically at the same level of care. Both needed feeding, dressing and toileting, neither could walk on their own, and coherent words were in short supply—but my son had now surpassed my mother: she was now on baby food, and he was chowing down on steak and vegies. He was playing sport, conversing constantly, and only occasionally needed a toilet reminder; she was non-verbal, couldn't voluntarily move, and had no control of bodily functions. The circle of life was in full swing in my universe . . . and cue that *Lion King* song playing in my head for the rest of the day.

In my mind this new dietary requirement for Mum was an obvious step towards the final, inevitable outcome. Dad, however, embraced it. Clearly it meant he could get more food into her, as she didn't need to chew it, so he was shovelling it in at record speed. At this stage of the disease, you would tend to start seeing a decline in body weight. Not for Mum—she was as healthy as an ox. Well, an ox that was slowly dying from Alzheimer's disease. Dad also took this as an opportunity to get as much coffee into her as he could. Dad loves his couple of lattes each day, so he would order two at a time, whack a straw in Mum's mouth and down the hatch. As long as her water intake was still adequate and it made Dad happy, then lattes all round. It wasn't as if all that caffeine was going to make her hyperactive, let's face it.

A few times I also caught him slipping a piece of chocolate into her mouth; he told me she enjoyed sucking on it, and it would dissolve in her mouth anyway. God bless him that he continued giving her all the things she enjoyed, whether it was the best dietary option or not. (For the record, if I am at some point put on a vitamised diet and can't feed myself, please just vitamise chocolate and give me plenty of it, and often.)

So once again, we were at a status quo. Mum's condition wasn't getting visibly worse, and this new dietary system was ensuring she was being fed adequately, and any major health issues were under control.

This is the point where you start to wonder how long somebody can physically continue in such a state. Short of a heart attack, or a devastating bout of influenza, or a fall (or technically a 'drop' in her case), Mum could have existed like that for another few years. I wasn't sure I was entirely comfortable with that, from a 'quality of life' point of view. What exactly was she getting out of life? We couldn't get her into her wheelchair anymore, so her world consisted of either sitting in her room or the communal area in the nursing home. To get from her bed to the living area, the carers had to use a body-lifting machine, which looked pretty uncomfortable to be strapped into. She couldn't talk, couldn't walk, couldn't recognise anyone, and most likely wasn't enjoying her food—what kind of life was that? What would she have said to us, if she could talk? What would she have wanted us to do? It becomes very taxing on your mind and your soul and your conscience. There were days I wished that phone call would come and it would all be over—for her sake, and then, selfishly, for all our sakes. We all knew she wasn't going to make a miraculous recovery from this disease, so the outcome was inevitable. But as much as these thoughts consumed me, the alternative was that I would never get to see her again, to hold her hand, to tell her I love her. So it was business as usual and we visited as often as we could, and supported Dad in every way we could, and accepted that he'd be by her side until the very end—whenever that may be.

Around that time, one of my best friends was diagnosed with stage-three bowel cancer. She was my age, and had a son the same age as mine—and until the day she called me with her 'news', my life had seemed pretty unfair. It's amazing how quickly life can put things in perspective. When she began undergoing treatment, I was her designated chemo buddy. Spending hours on end in a cancer ward is rather humbling, to say the least. Cancer can strike anyone, of any age, at any time. Much of the talk that takes place in chemo wards is about 'getting through this' and 'fighting this disease'. Of course there is inoperable and incurable cancer, but there is often an element of hope as well. Hope for relief. Hope for remission. Hope for a cure.

Those of us who have or have had a loved one with Alzheimer's know that there is currently no cure for the disease. No treatment, no holistic medicines, no lifestyle changes can either reverse or cure it. Given that it primarily affects the older generation, there is almost an element of acceptance about it. We joke about having it, and deep down many of us probably fear actually succumbing to it at some point. Once something is seen as inevitable, it becomes easier to joke about it; we aren't just tempting fate anymore, it's a fait accompli.

I wonder how that will all change when a cure is found.

21

Timing is everything

I had started working on a new television project and was putting in ten to twelve hour days. Those hours were not unusual when I was working on a show; it becomes all-consuming, both mentally and physically. I had spent most of my life freelancing in the world of television, moving from show to show, with periods of time off in between productions, which suited my lifestyle perfectly. I was able to afford the luxury of immersing myself in a show, knowing I'd have a month or so off at the other end. My husband had been playing the role of Mr Mum perfectly, but as my mother deteriorated, he was also having to pick up the slack with Dad, fielding the nightly phone calls and then relaying the latest news when I returned home that night.

One Monday evening I got home around 11 p.m. Exhausted, I sat down in the living room to catch up on the daily news.

My husband told me Dad had called to say Mum wasn't doing that well—she wasn't very interested in food and would barely open her eyes. Nothing out of the usual, so I just assumed she was a bit off colour, or had picked up a bug.

Early the next morning, before heading into the office, I gave Dad a call. He sounded his usual positive self—but also a bit worried that he couldn't get any food into Mum, and that anything he did manage to get into her mouth just sat there. I suggested he chat with her carers and maybe ask a nurse to do a bit of a check-up.

So off I went to work, and gave Dad a call in the afternoon. Mum was still the same, but the nurse didn't think there was anything sinister going on—she had no infections or illness that required treatment, so they'd keep monitoring her and hopefully she would start eating again tomorrow. My husband would be conversing with Dad, then updating me via text message.

I should explain at this point that after our son was born, my husband and I took a few years off work so we could both be full-time parents. Our son was a long time coming, and was going to be our only child, so we felt it was important to not miss out on anything. I went back to full-time work first, and it was then I realised that I had married a very thorough man. Because we were both so invested in our child, my husband fell into the habit of texting me several times during the day with a quick update on our child's activities—'he just woke up', 'just had lunch', 'rolled over', 'had a poo'. These text messages would appear on my phone frequently, but from a desire to not be looking at my phone ten times during a meeting, I occasionally didn't get to read them until later in the day.

During that day, a few 'no change with your mum', 'still hasn't eaten anything' text messages came through from my husband. (I'm glad 'just had a poo' wasn't one of them—that might have tipped me over the edge.) At home that night, my husband said he'd chatted with Dad, and Mum still hadn't eaten anything.

The next morning, after a restless sleep, I rang Dad and he agreed to keep me in the loop about Mum's condition. As the executive producer of a live television show, Wednesday was show day, and as they say in the very glamorous world of show business, the show must go on—so I had no option but to go to work. I tried calling Dad a few times throughout the day, but his phone kept going to voicemail, which wasn't unusual, as he couldn't figure out how to work his mobile at the best of times.

At about 4 p.m. my husband called me; the nursing home staff, who had also been consulting with the nurse, had come to the conclusion that Mum had now fully lost her ability to swallow. This basically left us with two options. We could either give them permission to start administering liquid food intravenously—or we could stop feeding Mum and place her on palliative care.

As that last sentence registered in my brain, I was being called into the studio for our show rehearsals. I stood in my office for a couple of minutes collecting my thoughts. Neither of those options were good ones. We had to make a decision on whether we wanted Mum to pass away soon, or sooner. I wasn't even sure what palliative care really entailed, but I ascertained from my husband that we could make the decision tomorrow, so I went off to rehearsals.

For the next few hours I was in show mode, making decisions about whether a fart gag was the best way to end a comedy sketch. One of the writers pleading his case actually said, 'Come on, trust me, it will *kill*.' Well, buddy, you know what would actually kill? Not feeding someone—but is it more humane to do it slowly while drip-feeding them over a few months, or do you do just stop feeding and then, before you know it, bang, they're gone. But my job at that moment was to make a decision about a fart joke—a decision that seemed so trivial compared to the one I should have been making. We had a live show going to air in less than an hour, so I had to pretend my head was in the game, and in the end I pulled off one of the greatest compartmentalised performances of my life. I think it was a good show—we went with the fart gag and it *did* kill.

The next morning I called in sick and drove to the nursing home to meet with Dad, my sister and the nursing staff—but not before quickly Googling 'palliative care'. I knew it had something to do with caring for someone in the later stages of life, but I needed to be versed with a bit more knowledge. I learnt that in a medical setting, it does indeed relate to end-of-life care, where the objective is to relieve pain and discomfort, rather than treat the underlying cause. In other words, palliative care aims to comfort, not cure. So for patients in the final stages of a terminal illness, the course of action is to make them as comfortable and as pain free as possible, until the time comes for them to pass in peace. For the family and carers, palliative care concentrates on providing emotional and practical support before and through the death of their loved one.

We walked into the nursing home manager's office and sat down. Nobody spoke for what seemed like an eternity. We were told that Mum had reached the stage where her body was shutting down. We had the option of having a drip put in and feeding Mum intravenously, which could keep her alive indefinitely, or until another condition took over—or we could stop feeding her, administer morphine to ensure she was comfortable, and allow her to pass peacefully in her own time. Decisions don't come much more intense than that.

I asked how long 'her own time' was likely to be; we were told it could be anywhere from two days to two weeks. I tried to get more of a definitive time line from her.

'So,' I persisted, 'do you think it will be two days, or will it be two weeks?'

'It's hard to tell,' said the nursing home manager, 'as it depends on the individual.'

My mind was racing. What did I have planned for the next two weeks? There was work, of course, which I would just have to deal with, but what about social functions—did my son have any birthday parties coming up? If it happened on a weekend, I wouldn't have to worry about work or getting our son to and from school . . . but then sometimes it's harder to get things done on a weekend. Why can't they just give us a more accurate time line than somewhere between two days and two weeks—was there an average?

And when it was time, would we get a 24-hour warning, or will it just happen out of the blue?

We were reassured we would know when the end was near, and there'd be plenty of time for us to make sure we were with her.

Well, that was a relief—after thirteen years, I'd hate to miss the actual moment. That would be like staying up all night for Santa, and he arrives just as you fall asleep. Not really, of course—but disappointing all the same.

We asked a few more questions, before leaving the office. I wasn't sure of the appropriate exiting gesture after a meeting like this—to say thank you, or shake hands, or a kiss on the cheek? It all seemed a little awkward to be honest.

Right—there we have it. Thirteen years of dealing with this and it now comes down to two weeks . . . maximum. I was pretty convinced Mum would fight as long as she could to stick around, so I felt like we had a bit of time to deal with this—to get our heads around it and prepare for what we had essentially been preparing for our whole lives.

We went to Mum's room and sat down with Dad. I could tell from his face that he had decided it was time. She really had suffered enough, and it was time to let her go.

I avoiding looking at Mum because deep down, part of me was feeling guilty that we had the power to end her life. We had spent so long hoping for some kind of sign or moment of recognition from her, and now I was too scared to look just in case she *did* open her eyes. What if she *could* actually hear what we were talking about, and was trying to give us a sign that she wasn't ready? Something in my brain was still telling me that maybe a miracle might occur, and if she could just hold on for a while longer, then . . . what? What could possibly happen to change the outcome of this incurable disease? Is there anything we could have done differently? Could we have tried harder to keep her brain active? Should we have spent more time with her in the nursing home? Should we have done more research into fighting this disease? I definitely should have told her way more often that I loved her. My mind was full of nonsense and I couldn't think straight. I was a blubbering mess. I was meant to be the strong one who handled things in a calm and calculated manner, but at the age of 47, I was having my 84-year-old father comfort me, saying, 'It's time, it's time.'

I finally got the courage to sit next to Mum and hold her hand. I just sat there and didn't speak. I was looking out of the window with the sun streaming through—it was a very peaceful and beautiful moment. I was wondering what Mum would have thought about all of this. How would she have handled it?

I was only twelve when my nana passed away. During the last few months of her life, my parents kept me from seeing her, as she was sedated and basically just wasting away in a hospital bed. The night my nana passed I had just gotten into bed, probably contemplating which Bay City Roller I was going to marry, when the phone rang and Dad answered. I couldn't hear what he was saying, but the conversation was short. He hung up, walked into the kitchen and said to Mum, 'She's gone.'

What I heard next has stuck with me all those years, and was something I could never really understand until that moment when I was holding my own mother's hand in the nursing home. Mum had said to Dad, 'That's a relief.'

Mum knew what it was like to battle this disease. She had battled it with her own mother, and was now about to succumb to her own battle with it. Would she have been relieved to be free of it? Would she have been horrified to think her own family had just made a decision to put her on palliative care?

As I sat there, holding her hand, I was hoping she would just give my hand a little squeeze, or open her eyes just to tell us that everything was okay, and that we were making the right decision.

She didn't.

22

It all comes down to this

The rest of that day was a bit of a blur. When I got home I sat down and made a list of all the people I needed to update on the situation. Mum was such a wonderful friend and auntie to so many people who would want to see her before she left us. The first phone call was to my cousin, who as a kid spent a lot of time with my parents. She went on holidays with us, and spent weekends at our house, and often referred to Mum as her 'other mother', but not in that rap 'sista from another mother' kind of way.

When she answered the phone, I managed to say 'hi', and that was it. She knew something was wrong, and was trying to get information out of me, repeatedly asking if Dad was okay. Odd, isn't it? Mum had been sick and dying for so long that most people never really expected anything to really happen to her, and were more worried about how Dad was faring. When I told Dad how people were asking about him, his response was, 'I should bloody go down and buy a lotto ticket because it seems I am lucky to be alive.'

I wanted to spend as much time as I could by Mum's side, but needed to go into work the next day for a quick script meeting. The distraction would be good for me. I got up early and headed to the nursing home to see how Mum was, and how Dad was holding up. He was going to have to sit there for the next two days to two weeks just watching his wife slip away.

When I arrived, it became obvious that word had got around—I couldn't go more than two metres without being hugged. Mum had been there so long, ever since the nursing home had first opened, and was like part of the furniture—and just like us, her nursing home family were having a tough time dealing with the inevitable. They were about to lose someone they had cared for over the past six years—and they would also be losing Dad, too. As much as he could be a daily pain in their arses, he was also part of their family, and losing both Mum *and* Dad would have a huge impact on the people in that building.

The nursing home had a different feel about it that day. Carers walking around would normally be buzzing past, throwing comments at Dad and stopping for a chat. But not that day. It was quiet and sombre. People were just looking over and giving a smile that basically said, 'I know what has happened and I am sorry, and if I come over to chat we will all probably cry, so I'll just go about my business if that's okay with you.' Even the residents seemed to be a bit less crazy that day.

When I eventually got to the communal living area, Mum was sitting in her usual chair, in her usual spot by the window. Dad was right next to her, holding her hand—as he had been for the past six years. I'm not sure what I expected to see, but the normality of the scene was quite weird. Dad said she'd had an uneventful night's sleep, and had her eyes open for a little while just before I arrived. Dad was looking very stoic and was virtually pushing me out the door to go to work: he had it all under control, and there was nothing I could do. I certainly sensed that he just wanted to be alone and quiet with Mum—to spend as much quality time with her as he could—and I wasn't about to begrudge him that.

As I pulled into the car park at work I took a few deep breaths and mentally prepared myself for my meeting. I entered my office to find an enormous bunch of flowers on my desk, and by the time I turned around a semicircle of colleagues had gathered outside my door, most of them offering that same smile I had seen in the nursing home that morning. It must be a universal look that we all use when we don't know the appropriate thing to say. It turned out that my assistant had called my husband to see if I was okay, thinking I'd seemed a bit distracted during Wednesday night's show— and all this time I thought I'd been master of my emotions.

Still, I remained fairly composed, and tried to play down the situation, saying words like 'Mum', 'palliative care', 'couple of weeks', 'all good, not sad'. I needed to focus to get through the meeting; the only trouble was that my face wasn't matching my brain, and I have absolutely no idea what was said for the next 90 minutes. If felt almost disrespectful to Mum for me to be sitting in a room with a group of people laughing at jokes and video clips, but there must have been moments when I forgot about what was occurring in a quiet communal living room a 45-minute drive away because I *did* manage to laugh that afternoon. For all I really remember of that day, I could've approved a three-legged dog reading a newsbreak. (Note to self: that would probably be a ratings bonanza!)

Meeting over, I announced to my team that it would be best for the show if I took a bit of time off, as I was probably only going to be a liability for the next week or so.

Okay, so joke hat off, grieving daughter hat back on as I headed back to see my dying mother.

Situation still normal at the nursing home. A few visitors were sitting around chatting with Dad as I sat with Mum, holding her hand. Every now and then Dad would get up and walk over to Mum with a drink, push a straw into her mouth and ask her to have a sip. I knew she couldn't swallow, so when she started coughing it was no real surprise. Dad said he hadn't managed to get anything into her all day.

At this point I was confused. Last time I checked, we had made the decision to stop feeding Mum and allow her body to shut down peacefully. I wasn't sure how to broach the topic of 'not feeding' with Dad, but I had to say something.

'I don't think we should be giving her anything, Dad, as she can't swallow, and she could choke.'

'Well, if we don't feed her, she is going to just die,' he answered.

'Dad, we agreed that we were going to stop feeding her.'

'Well, I just don't think we can sit here and not try to keep her alive. I'm not sure we've made the right decision.'

'I think we *did* make the right decision, Dad—but if you want to change your mind, then it is totally up to you and we will not question it.'

As I gently tried to remind him of the decision we'd all made together, as a family, only two days before, I also remembered that this was a man who was ready to sign a 'DNR' form years ago. Good decision not to bring that one up.

I went to chat with the nurse on duty. She was aware Dad had been trying to give Mum liquids—and food, much to my horror—throughout the day. She told me that at this point it is very normal for family to question these kinds of decisions, as making a decision is often easy, but watching it being enforced is tough. Her advice was reassuring: Mum wasn't going to get much liquid through a straw anyway, so if it made Dad feel better about not starving her, then we should just let him do it.

So I was on board with the non-feeding but happy to watch Dad try to feed Mum plan. Still, it broke my heart every time

Dad got up to put that straw in her mouth. He was so devoted, even in those last days, and determined to do anything to keep the love of his life by his side.

I stayed for most of the afternoon, then headed home to get my son fed, bathed and into bed. The next day was Saturday and I wanted to take him to see his nana; the day after Saturday was Father's Day. I hadn't even thought about what to get Dad, or my husband—or gifts from my son to his Pa and dad. I was determined to make things as normal as possible, so once my son was in bed I went shopping for gifts. As I wandered around the mall a strange thing happened. For at least the past ten years, I had always walked around shopping centres with the curse of Mum's disease over my head. I was forever looking for gifts that would stimulate her or make her more comfortable—and these gifts were never easy to find. Every birthday, Christmas and Mother's Day would result in an unsuccessful hunt for just the right thing. As I meandered from shop to shop looking for Father's Day gifts, I kept seeing things that would have been perfect for Mum, but I didn't buy them—it was too late. Mum didn't need them anymore. It was all about to be over, and the consequences of that were having a ripple effect on everything I saw, did and thought. It was a very surreal shopping expedition, and I arrived home with nothing for Mum, Dad or my husband. Thankfully my son had a very interesting piece of artwork and an 'I love you Daddy' card that he had prepared at school earlier. He also managed to produce a 'Happy Father's Day Papa' card out of his bag. What a champ.

The next morning my husband, my son and I headed over to the nursing home. To keep things as normal as possible, I set up the coffee table with muffins and ordered lattes for everyone. We all sat around chatting and, from the point of view of a stranger wandering by, all was well in this little happy family scene—except that in this nursing home there were no strangers. Everybody knew the situation and was feeling the enormity of it, so we had many visits from passers-by expressing their condolences. My son knew something wasn't right. We hadn't told him his nana was dying; he was only five, so we knew he couldn't really understand the reality of it all. He did ask a few times why so many people were crying, so I told him Nana was a little sick and people were sad about that. He just shrugged his shoulders. To him, Nana had always been sick.

My sister arrived to take over the shift; we felt it was important for at least one of us to be with Dad. My brother was flat out at work, and with five adult children of his own, time was never on his side. He hadn't visited Mum for a few days, but was planning to see her and Dad on Father's Day, along with most of the family. Even though I had clearly failed to procure a gift for Dad, I wanted Father's Day to be special for him, and for everyone to be around him.

As I was sitting next to Mum, I could hear that her breathing was a little laboured. She didn't seem to be in any pain, but she had a bit of a chest infection, so the nurse was planning on setting up an oxygen mask for us to place over her mouth whenever she seemed to be struggling for breath. The oxygen mask was nothing new, as Mum had already had a few of these chest infections, so by the time we said our goodbyes, my sister and father had it all under control. Dad had decided to stay in Mum's room from now on, just so he could be there if anything happened, so we had set up a comfy area in her room where he could get a few hours sleep.

Mum's room was not very big. It had her bed, which was a hospital-style one with a big metal headboard and adjustable rails either side, and one of those moulded mattresses that kept her in position throughout the night. Next to her bed was an armchair that, judging from the indents in the seat, Dad spent many hours occupying. Her bed was parallel to a window that overlooked a paddock filled with sheep; Dad would've used that as the source of a joke more than once when the nurses came in at night to check on her. At the foot of the bed was a TV unit, which had a few baskets underneath filled with DVDs and books. The walls were adorned with family photos and a few printed canvases of orchids. She had a bathroom furnished with a shower, hand rails and a toilet with one of those potty chairs sitting over it. In real-estate terms it would have been described as a comfortable, modern one-bedroom studio with WIRs and a separate bathroom.

I gave Mum a kiss, told her I loved her and would see her in the morning. I also asked her not to give Dad any trouble as tomorrow was Father's Day and I didn't have a present for him.

She must not have heard me.

Early next morning, after a sleepless night, I was woken by a phone call from Dad. He sounded a little distressed, and said Mum had a terrible night, struggling on and off to breathe, but was now resting comfortably. I said I'd head over as soon as possible, but he told me not to panic as she was 'good as gold' at the moment, and just to head over when we were ready for our Father's Day brunch at 10 a.m.

I called my sister to update her and also reiterated that Dad said not to rush up as Mum seemed pretty comfortable. I called my brother, and as it turned out he was getting an early start and was already on his way up there. After going over the day's list of things to do in my head, I slowly extracted myself out of bed. I went into my son's room and got his clothes ready, then headed for the shower.

As I stood in the shower, steam filled the room and the hot water cascaded down my back. I remember thinking that we were likely to have a few restless nights over the next week or so as Mum started to go downhill. How bad was it likely to get? Would they just monitor her around the clock? I assumed Mum would want all of us there, gathered around her as a family, when she drew her last breath.

The shower screen door opened and broke my train of thought. I turned around and my husband was standing in front of me with my mobile phone.

'That was your brother,' he said.

'Let me guess—flat tyre?' My brother was renowned for having something go wrong at the most inopportune times.

'Your mum's gone.'

'Gone where?' I enquired, feeling very confused. They'd better not have taken her to a hospital without checking with us.

'She's gone.'

'What do you mean she's gone?' I asked again.

'She just passed away.'

'Oh,' I said.

I closed the shower screen door.

I still had conditioner in my hair, but there was no rush now. Mum had gone, so why did I need to rush.

I stood in the shower for another five minutes, making sure I got every last bit of conditioner out of my hair. That particular brand was not my favourite. It left my hair feeling a bit squeaky, so I really should get a bottle of the one with lavender in it that smells so nice and leaves my hair really soft and shiny.

Yes, that's exactly what I will do.

23

One last time

I drove to the nursing home alone. There was no point telling my son what had happened—Dad would mostly likely stay with us for the next few days, and the last thing he needed was a five-year-old asking questions about how dead Nana actually was.

I have no idea how I really got there, and how many red lights I may have driven through by the time I pulled into the car park.

Deep breath.

Near the front doors, next to the coffee shop, two carers were hugging each other, clearly distressed. I wonder what has happened, I thought to myself. As the doors opened they both walked over and embraced me and I realised it was my mum they were mourning. Strangely composed, I began comforting them for their loss. Then the woman who ran the cafe came out to see me. We'd spent many hours in that cafe and had become quite close to her. She hugged me and whispered in my ear, 'Your mum was a beautiful woman.' I tried to comfort her too, as best I could.

Comforting someone in a time of grief is a funny thing. I found I wasn't comfortable just sobbing on everyone's shoulder. In our family, crying had always been made fun of—not in a mean way, but in a teasing kind of way. Every time Mum cried, which was often, Dad would call out, 'Here come the waterworks!' and one of us would run to grab a box of tissues.

I had inherited my mother's ability to cry at the drop of a hat. We both wore our emotions on the surface and it didn't take much to set us off. I would tear up at the first sign of happiness, sadness, pain, you name it. It was a beautiful trait in her that she was so emotional—and then, being the hilarious family we were, we made fun of her for it. I'm embarrassed whenever I cry in public, so when I feel myself tearing up—which is often—I try to diffuse the situation with a joke or shut it down before it escalates to tears. On Mother's Days, and anniversaries of Mum's birthday or death, I find myself warning people not to be nice to me, or I'll cry. Maybe it's that old adage of 'once the floodgates open'.

Clearly I wasn't going to be able to cover up my emotions on this occasion, but I certainly wasn't laying them all out on the table. Maybe I was reserving them for an appropriate time. You hear about people not really crying about the death of a loved one until some time later, when the reality of the situation hits them.

I headed up to Mum's floor. As the elevator doors opened, I looked towards the communal living area, where I would have normally seen Mum sitting in her usual chair, in her usual spot by the window, with Dad holding her hand. It was empty.

I turned to walk down the corridor towards Mum's room; a group of people were standing outside her door. As I approached, one of them walked into Mum's room and came out with my dad in tow, followed by my brother. Dad walked towards me and we hugged. Neither of us were crying. I was waiting to hear him say those words my mother had said 35 years ago when her own mother passed, but they didn't come. It *wasn't* a relief for him. He *didn't* want it to end. He would have been happy to sit and hold her hand until they came and wheeled him out in a box.

We broke our embrace and I looked into his eyes. I was going to ask if he was okay, but figured it was probably a redundant question.

'Have you slept?' I asked.

'I've got plenty of time to sleep.'

'Have you eaten anything?'

'I'll get something later.'

'Do you have a clean shirt? That one has coffee on it.'

He looked down at his shirt. 'I'm saving that bit for later, for when the cafe is closed.'

What a guy. He could still throw out a one-liner an hour after his wife of 58 years had died.

We walked into a little room that was adjacent to Mum's. I gathered this was where families congregated in these situations—like a bereavement holding pen. There was a family pack of Arnott's assorted biscuits on the table and a box of tissues. An urn on the side bench was steaming away. What more would we possibly need at a time like this? Dad, my brother and I sat down at the table. I was eyeing off an orange cream biscuit just as my sister arrived. She was visibly upset, which set me off, which set Dad off, which set my brother off. Eventually we were all hugging and crying and sniffling and my desire for an orange cream was being marginally challenged by my need for a tissue.

We all sat and composed ourselves. I was the first to speak, asking my brother if he was there when it happened. He said he arrived around 9 a.m. and Mum was in bed, with Dad sitting next to her, holding her hand. He said she looked skeletal and diminished, but there was still a light in her eyes, and definitely a flicker of recognition. He leant down, hugged her, and told her he loved her and that everything was okay. As he stood back up her eyes followed him across the room. He said there wasn't a definitive moment when she left—no shudder, no noise, no last breath that he could discern—but within a minute or two just a total stillness. And then she was gone. He said her eyes were still open, and they were looking in Dad's direction, but the spark had vanished. Dad seemed unaware she had actually passed, so my brother left the room to find a nurse. She checked Mum and confirmed she had died. She seemed reluctant to pass on the news, as if not wanting to finally close the book of their long life together. When she did, it was quiet and respectful: 'She's gone, Frankie, she is at peace now.' Dad then leant down to say his last goodbyes. As he stood back up, my brother saw a look of bewilderment on Dad's face, almost childlike, as if he was wondering, what do I do now?

I had very mixed emotions about what I was hearing, and what had just happened. My sister and I had conducted virtually an around-the-clock bedside vigil with Mum, and the moment by brother walks in—bingo, she decided to let go. And of all days on Father's Day!

The only reasoning that made it sit okay with me was the thought that Mum was in control of that moment. She knew my sister and I had been by her side for all that time, and she was just holding on until my brother could make it. And she knew everyone would be around making a fuss of Dad that day, so it was the perfect time for her to leave us. That was the only possible scenario that made any sense to me, and didn't leave me feeling mad and frustrated and robbed of being there for those final moments. Maybe she knew my brother was tougher than me and my sister combined, and we wouldn't have actually coped being there at the end.

Dad was as calm and composed as I had seen him for a long time—maybe he had been waiting for my brother to arrive also?

I asked if I could go back into Mum's room and say goodbye. As I entered her room I could feel my body tensing up. I had never seen a dead body before, and had absolutely no idea what would be waiting for me on that bed. I instantly thought back to a scene in a movie I saw as a teenager, where a deceased body was lying in a bed, and then suddenly catapulted itself towards the person standing at the end. Was this possible—something to do with the soul leaving the body? I was pretty confident it was just an urban myth. Hoping it was anyway.

The first thing I saw was Mum lying on her back, propped up with a pillow, her eyes closed, her mouth slightly ajar. I'm glad her eyes were closed, as I didn't want to have to close them. I had seen this done so many times in movies, and had always wondered how they did it. Do a dead person's eyelids just close automatically as a reaction to being touched, or do you have to exert some pressure on the eyelids and actually pull them down with your hand? On telly it always seemed so smooth and easy.

Someone had placed a single yellow rose on her chest. Who did that? Did they have roses on hand for this specific reason? I knew they didn't sell them at the nursing home, but someone had put a yellow rose on her. That was nice.

I walked closer to the bed and just stood for a while looking at her—watching to see if she really wasn't breathing. I leant down to brush the hair off her forehead so I could kiss her. I touched her skin and pulled my hand back in fright: she was stone-cold! That feeling of her cold skin almost sent me running out of the room in shock. Although it made sense for her body to be cold—and I have heard and used the saying 'the body wasn't even cold yet'—I wasn't expecting her body to actually be cold. She had passed no less than an hour ago—how could her body be so cold so soon? And so still and quiet? No sound, no movement, no twitching. Nothing. I struggled with that.

As I touched her forehead again, I instantly felt like that wasn't my mother lying there. I had been too late, she had left us. Maybe if her skin had still been warm I would have felt like part of her had remained. Is there something in the thought that it takes a while for the soul to leave the body? If so, hers had gone. I had really wanted to be there to hold her hand while she took her final breath. I wanted to tell her how much I loved her and how she was the best mother in the world and that I would miss her every day for the rest of my life. But she was cold. I would never get to tell her those things because she was cold.

I bent down and kissed her cheek, then sat down to tell her everything I needed to. All of those things I should have told her the night before but didn't, because she wasn't meant to die that morning.

I left her room and walked back into the bereavement area. We all just sat there dazed for a while, until the nursing home manager came in to talk business. She gave us all big hugs, conveyed her sadness for our loss, and then asked if we had a funeral home in mind. I ordinarily would have used the line

'The body is not even cold yet' but it was, so on to the next thing, I guess.

For thirteen years we knew this day was coming, for the past six years we could see it coming, and for the past four days it was upon us—but not one of us had talked about this post-death stuff. We had never mentioned a funeral, had never talked about cremation or burial. In fact Mum and Dad's will hadn't even been looked at in over 30 years. What was that about? Why hadn't we as a family talked about this? Is that denial at its best, or is that normal? I see those pre-planned funeral ads on television and think to myself, who goes in and pre-plans their funeral? Who invests in a funeral plan? Obviously people a little more realistic and organised than us. I didn't have the first clue as to what to do or who to call. Did Mum have to go to a hospital to be declared deceased, or did she just go straight to a funeral home? It was a Sunday— and Father's Day at that—so would funeral homes even be open today? Did we need a priest? Did we need to put some clothes on her? She was still in her nightie and had a yellow rose on her chest. Do her false teeth go with her? My head was swimming and I still couldn't get over how cold she was.

I sat down and ate that elusive orange cream biscuit, just to clear my head.

There was a funeral home on the corner of my street that I passed at least twice a day, but at that moment I couldn't for the life of me remember what it was called. I have always had this weird suspicion when driving past funeral homes that if I look at them, it's a sign that I will end up there. Makes absolutely no sense, but I've always avoided them like the plague. Luckily my sister is not as unhinged as me and she remembered its name. Apparently funeral home staff are on call 24/7, even on Father's Day, so the nursing home arranged for them to come and collect Mum.

It felt like less than ten minutes had gone by before I looked up to see an empty trolley being wheeled past the doorway and into Mum's room. I asked Dad if he wanted to go back in to see Mum one last time, but he declined. He had said his goodbyes and was at peace with how he left it. He probably got to say everything he needed to say while she was still warm. Good for him. I was still feeling a little cheated.

As we sat there waiting for them to bring Mum out, I started to get a little agitated. I was stressing about looking up and seeing the trolley come out of her room with her lying on it and a sheet over her head. Surely they wouldn't have one of those little tags tied to her toe with string, would they? I didn't want that to be the final image of my mother that stayed in my head forever. Thankfully, just as they were bringing the trolley out, a curtained screen was slid across the doorway to our room and we were shielded from her final exit. I wondered whether that curtained screen belonged to the funeral home or the nursing home, and was it called the 'death curtain', or did it serve other purposes as well? Did they have different sizes in case you are wheeling a body past double doors? It resembled that green curtain in *The Wizard of Oz*, but it was beige instead of green. Beige seems to the most inoffensive colour when dealing with death.

•

The rest of that day just kind of happened, with me feeling like I was in some removed state of mind. Pretty sure I went home and crashed for a bit. Dad would be staying at our house for a while, so it was going to be a game of smoke and mirrors to shield my son from what had just happened. Pa arriving at our house on a Sunday was enough to cause a certain level of suspicion, but we just kept up the story that Nana was a bit sick so Pa would be staying with us for a while.

Soon the flowers started arriving, the phone didn't stop ringing, and we were in full mourning mode. The funeral home was in my street, so it seemed logical to use my house as base camp for the next few days while we got stuff sorted. It was weird knowing that Mum was just a few doors up in that funeral home, possibly lying on a trolley, and who knew what they were doing with her in a post-death, pre-funeral kind of way. Were they being gentle with her? Do they refer to her by name, or is she just a number in a group of bodies they have lying around? It's been two years since Mum passed, and I often walk past that funeral home twice a day and still my mind conjures up all kinds of crazy scenarios.

I love a good event to organise, and Mum's funeral was going to be a beauty. Granted, I had no idea where to start, as I had only been to three funerals in my life, and all were utterly different. One was for a roommate from England, who committed suicide; only her father and brother had flown out to Australia for her funeral, attended by my parents and another friend—so, pretty low-key and tragic. The next funeral was for my aunt, Mum's sister. There were lots of family and friends, and at the end of the service, they draped her coffin in a Collingwood Football Club flag and played the club theme song; even Mum wasn't as committed to the Collingwood cause as her sister! The last was for a close friend who had survived cancer for many years, but lost her battle with the disease at the age of 32. She was a public figure, so her funeral was bigger than *Ben-Hur*—the full-meal deal with news crews and security. Pretty certain Mum's send-off was going to pale in comparison to that one.

The first order of business was to discuss our options and wishes with the funeral home. Walking into the building felt a bit freaky: so much time had passed leading up to this event, but not a single moment's thought had gone into it. I found myself shaking the director's hand and saying, 'Nice to meet you.' Actually, it wasn't nice to meet him. I wish I didn't *have* to meet him, but I didn't know what else to say. My brother, sister and I sat down at a round table and agreed on a day and a time for the funeral. The celebrant we requested wasn't available, so the funeral home suggested another celebrant, who ironically was a former actor in a soap opera that Mum used to watch religiously—so it seemed rather fitting that he would preside over the ceremony. Mum loved a good celebrity sighting, so that would have made her very happy. We talked about flowers and, given our parents' love of growing orchids, decided on a nice bouquet of orchids to adorn the coffin. And the coffin—how does one go about choosing a coffin? I wasn't too fired up about the idea of walking into their coffin showcase room and neither was my sister, so my brother gallantly volunteered to choose one, following the funeral director through a doorway while my sister and I stayed behind talking about whether Mum would like a white coffin with gold accessories, or something a little more neutral. We got through about two options and my brother walked back into the room.

'All done,' he announced proudly, and sat back down.

'That was quick!' my sister said in surprise.

'Well, I just went with the first and cheapest one I could find—there's no use spending a ton of money on a coffin, is there? And besides, it will be covered in flowers.'

My brother had a point, but I was a little stunned at the efficiency of his decision. He was clearly operating on autopilot and emotions were just going to get in the way. In hindsight I guess it was good to have a family member make a rational decision and not prolong the process agonising over choices of colours and finishes, or whether Mum would have preferred gold or silver handles.

We looked through some order-of-service booklet examples and decided that as I had a graphic design background, I would design the booklet myself and send the artwork through to the printer. We were saving money all over the place here! We then talked about readings. My brother wanted to do the eulogy, and his youngest son wanted to talk on behalf of the grandkids. My sister and I decided we would read a poem together for moral support. We decided against a video or photo collage tribute, but to instead to keep it all quick and simple with a few songs and meaningful words.

Let's see how much this send-off is going to cost, then.

After a few minutes of punching numbers into the calculator, and a few 'we can factor a bit of a discount in there' comments, he left the room to print out the breakdown of costs, before sliding the printout across the table for us to look at.

So, that will be FIVE MILLION DOLLARS! All that was missing was the funeral director's pinky finger placed at the corner of his mouth.

It's not as if we were going to say, 'Well, we'll have a think, maybe shop around, and get back to you.' They had Mum as collateral.

It's very much like buying a car; there are tons of extras that add up—beige interior, sunroof (maybe not a good idea for a coffin), gloss exterior, shiny accessories . . .

Will that be cash or credit card today?

•

I hit the ground running; there was so much to do. Music to choose, photos to find, a frame to buy for the photo of Mum on the coffin, artwork to prepare for the order of service, catering to organise for the afterparty at my house, and invitations to send out. I actually sat down to start working on an invitation, and then remembered people don't send out invites for a funeral. You just put a notice in the paper and then word would just get around. Well, that was one less job to do.

I spent a whole day choosing photos. Mum and Dad were always the life of the party, and I found plenty of goofy shots from their time together, some of which Mum would have been horrified at having on public display. I chose a beautiful photo taken about a year before she started to go downhill, showing her at her best—big smile, sparkling eyes and a beautiful complexion that defied her years. Mum was always a classic beauty, and up until the day she passed her face had barely a wrinkle on it. (I am lucky enough to have inherited her complexion—pale skin and freckles. I spent many a weekend in the bathroom using lemon juice and bleach on my skin trying to get rid of those damn freckles. And if I had a dollar for every person who said 'If you joined them all up you would have a great tan', I would be rich and then I could afford to have that skin-bleaching surgery that worked so well on Michael Jackson. But I also inherited a susceptibility to skin cancer. Two years ago I had a skin cancer removed from my temple, and the dermatologist confirmed that this is going to be my lot in life. I spend way too much time thinking that if the skin cancer doesn't get me, the Alzheimer's will.)

I printed out the photo and slipped it into a lovely gold-painted wooden frame. It looked so nice I decided to place it on the mantelshelf in the lounge room for a few days before I took it up to the funeral home, with a small bunch of flowers next to it as a tribute.

That day, when my son arrived home from school, he called out for me to come in and look at something. He was sitting on the couch in the lounge room and had turned the television on. He looked up at the picture of Mum and said, 'Why is that picture of Nana up there?'

'Well, Nana has been very sick, and I thought it would be nice to put a photo of her up there, so every time we look at it we think about her,' I answered.

'Did Nana die?' he asked, not taking his eyes off the photo.

Okay, so I knew this conversation was coming, but I was hoping we could get through the funeral first. Through all the raw emotions still on the surface.

'Well, darling, she *did* die, because she had been very sick for a long time, and it was time for her leave us.'

Still he was looking at the photo and although his eyes didn't move, I could see that they were welling up, and his bottom lip was starting to protrude. I put my arm around him.

'It's okay to be sad, buddy, you know Nana loved you very much.'

He then started to actually cry, and turned to put his head into my shoulder.

'I know you are going to miss Nana, mate, but she will always be with you.'

I managed to extract his head from my shoulder and look him in the eye. He was trying to compose himself, and took a breath in before he spoke.

'I'm going to miss her wheelchair!' he sobbed.

I did a pretty good job of not laughing or dismissing his genuine feeling of loss—albeit for the wheelchair, not his nana.

'Well, we still have her wheelchair, so you can have a ride in it anytime you like.'

He turned his head away, and looked back at the photo on the mantel. Then his gaze shifted back down to the TV. 'Hey look!' he said. 'That's Alvin from *Alvin and the Chipmunks*.' He bounced up on his feet, happily walked out of the lounge room, and we were done.

I was glad to be spared all the questions I had feared were coming—where is Nana now, is she in heaven, can she see us, can she hear us? These were all questions I was grappling with myself. I think my son was possibly the perfect age to face a death in the family. From that day on he spoke of Nana in the past tense, so he clearly understood she was no longer with us. He had a certain amount of sadness that she had gone away, but perhaps didn't quite comprehend the emotional loss or the finality of it all. His relationship with her had never been quality one-on-one time spent talking and playing. There really wasn't anything about Nana that he was going to miss—except for her wheelchair, of course. He did, however, realise that her death had affected everyone else in the house, so he took it upon himself to check in on everyone's state of emotions as often as possible. He would constantly ask if I was missing my mum, and ask my dad if he was sad that Nana was dead. There was no way any of us could let our minds forget even for a moment what was happening. He was always ready to snap us back into reality.

As I was attempting to get him into bed that night, he was not very cooperative. As he finally lay down, I asked him for a hug and he declared that he was now too tired to hug me. I sat down on the side of his bed and told him that I wished I could hug my mum one last time but I can't. I heard my husband walk up behind me and ask me to step outside for a moment. I thought he was going to step in and talk our son around, explain to him that this would be a really nice opportunity to make his mum happy when she was clearly very sad. As we stood outside his door, my husband looked at me and said in no uncertain terms, 'It's too early to play the dead mum card'.

I was shocked. How dare he say that to me. How dare he accuse me of using a recent traumatic event in my life to my advantage and in turn use it to force my son into performing an act he clearly wasn't in the mood for? The problem here was that he was absolutely right. I had just lost my mum and I wanted my own child to hug me—and if I wanted to play that card, then that's exactly what I would do. I continue to play that card occasionally right up until this day. I've earnt that card and it's my right to play it whenever I choose. Don't judge me. I walked back into that room and got my hug, although I had a sneaking suspicion that even my son knew the score that night.

The next morning I decided to go into work to take care of the emails that were piling up in my inbox. A few hours at work would clear my head—and I could access the music library while I was there. More flowers greeted me on my desk, and everyone was very supportive, but also a little surprised to see me there the day before Mum's funeral—I just mumbled something about how cathartic is was to be around friends.

At my desk I started searching for music tracks that might be appropriate for a funeral ceremony. Whenever you use music in a television show you must pay a nominal amount to the performer and writer and record company for its use—and often obtain permission, depending on how you will use the music. Did you have to do that funerals? Are there musicians sitting around deciding whether to grant permission for someone to be farewelled by their song? Do some musicians purposely write a song hoping that someone will choose it for a funeral? Whoever wrote 'Wind Beneath My Wings' must be high-fiving at the current world mortality rate. I had no idea what the protocol was here.

As I looked around my office, I admired the makeshift florist that was rapidly growing there and thought it might be a nice gesture to send some flowers to Mum's nursing home.

They, like our family, were grieving, and I wanted to show how much we appreciated all the care and support they had given Mum and Dad over the past six years. I called a florist and told them I'd like a nice bright arrangement—somewhere around the one hundred dollar mark. When they asked what message I would like on the card, it all turned pear shaped. I managed to utter, 'To our dear friends at . . .' and then couldn't speak at all. The voice at the other end was trying to prompt me, but I couldn't say a word. My throat was tight, I could barely breathe and I felt light-headed. I hung up the phone as my assistant came in to my rescue. Perhaps coming in to work wasn't the smartest idea I'd ever had, but I didn't foresee that something as simple as ordering flowers would have such a profound effect. I managed to scribble down some notes for my assistant, who mercifully took care of it all for me.

I checked out of the office for the rest of the week and headed home to continue with the funeral planning. I needed to talk to Dad about the music. Mum had passed three days before, and the most he had managed to do was sit on the couch in the lounge room in his dressing gown and doze on and off. I think it was hard for him seeing us up and about, going about our business. His world as he knew it had ended, and assimilating back into normal life wasn't going to be easy. He was definitely struggling with the fact that we weren't outwardly paralysed by sadness and grief, but the truth was, we had been grieving for years, as the woman we knew had left us years ago. It was as if he now had nothing to do, nobody who needed him, nowhere to be. All of this buzzing about around him was making him very grumpy, and every time I started to get frustrated, I had to take a deep breath and put myself in his slippers (his desired footwear of the moment) and make him feel part of the arrangements.

Dad and I talked about what songs were significant to them throughout their marriage. We all knew Mum's favourite song was 'Somewhere Over the Rainbow' by Judy Garland, so Dad was happy for that to be the first song of the service. Even while Mum was alive and well, we always knew that we'd use that song at her funeral one day—which made it completely impossible for me to hear it without bursting into tears. At their wedding 58 years prior, they had played 'Because' by Mario Lanza, so that seemed an appropriate choice to slip in somewhere. Then my sister and I started talking about what songs we would hear Mum regularly sing along to. Doris Day's 'Que Sera, Sera' was one we agreed on. I knew the words to that song before I could walk, and whenever I heard it I always thought of Mum happily swaying along in the kitchen while doing whatever she was doing. It would be nice as the final song of the ceremony, leaving everyone with a happy piece of music as they farewelled our mum. I floated the idea of having the words appear on the video screen with a bouncing ball, but Dad shut that one down pretty quickly.

'I don't want you turning this into a bloody circus.'

Note to self—cancel the elephants and acrobats!

24

The final curtain

The morning of the funeral, I woke with a sense of purpose. This was going to be a tough day, but we were going to get through it as a family. My husband took our son off to school (sorry, I am not a fan of kids at funerals) while I got myself and Dad dressed and fed before heading over to the funeral home to set some things up. When I returned my sister and brother had arrived, and an hour before the service we were all sitting around my kitchen table laughing, even Dad. It was like we were all avoiding the emotion that was about to take over —and the moment I looked up at the clock and said it was time to head out, the mood changed. It was a sombre walk up to the end of the street, and we all stopped before we walked inside. I turned to Dad, who was looking very composed, and put my hands on his shoulders.

'Today is a celebration of Mum's life—let's think about all the happiness she brought to this world, and to everyone she met, and send her off with a smile.'

At which point I started to cry. Dad grabbed my hands and gave them a squeeze. He was as calm and stoic as I had seen him in a long time.

'Come on, Shelley,' he said, 'no tears today.'

Of course him saying that ensured there *were* tears.

We stood as a family at the entrance to the funeral home and started to welcome the guests in. It was so comforting to see friends from my childhood I hadn't seen in years—all of my friends loved my mum and it was evident today that she was a popular woman. Dad was amazing, shaking hands, hugging, kissing babies—very presidential.

Everyone started to make their way inside and take their seats. We all sat in the front row, Dad between my sister and me, with my husband next to me on the end. I sat there saying to myself over and over, 'Don't cry, Don't' cry,' and when Dad offered a hand to each of his girls, to help us through the bumpy ride ahead, I laughed and said, 'Here come the waterworks'—and of course started crying.

I looked down at the order of service. Why had we decided to start with 'Somewhere Over the Rainbow'? There was no coming back from the emotion of that song, and at some point I would need to be composed enough to do a reading with my sister. Now I will never be able to watch *The Wizard of Oz*, a movie my son loves, ever again. We should have chosen something less emotional, maybe something instrumental without words. But then somebody pressed the play button and 'Somewhere Over the Rainbow' was off and running.

And then there was the brown wooden coffin with the silver handles, sitting only ten feet away, with my mother's deceased body lying inside. I couldn't look at it, and wished it wasn't there. I was expecting a white coffin and she was much more a gold person than silver, and the frame that held her photo was gold edged, so it clashed quite badly with the design my brother had selected. What were we thinking? We really should have coordinated that better. And what happens to the coffin after the ceremony? Mum was to be cremated, and I had not spent a single moment in my life thinking about what happens to coffins when people are cremated. Do they recycle and resell them? Does the coffin go into the furnace—and if so, how much of the ashes would be Mum, and how much would be wood? And how do the silver (not gold) handles work in an urn—surely they would just melt? These were the thoughts that were running through my head while Judy Garland's voice filled the room, to the accompaniment of sniffles coming from somewhere behind me.

The celebrant walked up to the podium and welcomed everyone to the service. He started off with some nice words and a few anecdotes about my mother that we'd shared with him over coffee earlier that week. If Mum was sitting next to me, she would have leant in and whispered, 'Is that so and so from that old television show?'; I wondered if anyone else had recognised him from that popular soap opera. Still I couldn't look at the coffin and instead became fixated on the program in my hands. I wasn't entirely happy with the font I had chosen—it might have been a bit flowery for such a solemn occasion. I wondered if there was a special funeral font designed just for this type of thing. Not too flowery, not too bold, and definitely not too Comic Sans.

I was startled out of my font deliberation by my brother standing up and heading to the podium. He is the kind of guy that keeps his emotions in check. Always the life of the party and the joke teller—a lot like Dad in so many ways—but I could see he was going to struggle with this. I was hoping he would get through it all, because if he lost it, then I was *really* going to lose it.

He started by talking about what it was like to be a kid in our family. Everyone felt loved and safe, and our house was always full of friends and family, having loads of laughs and loads of cake. He talked about cake quite a bit in his five-minute spot, and kept the congregation laughing as much as he could. Every time he started getting emotional, he brought it back with a zinger. He even managed to throw in a 'my sister was adopted' joke and I actually started laughing at the surprised whispers that rippled through the crowd. Then, finally, it got to him. Halfway through a sentence he stopped. He looked down, cleared his throat, and tried to speak again. Nothing. It was really hard to see him up there in such a raw state. If he couldn't get through his bit, what hope did my sister and I have up there?

My nephew was next up and his memories about the best nana in the world were doing nothing to moderate my emotions. He also talked quite a bit about cake.

Then it was our turn. My sister generously leant over and offered to go it alone if I wasn't up for it, but I needed to do this. My sister had selected a poem called 'She is Gone', by English painter and poet David Harkins. I still can't manage to read it without sobbing.

We made it through, sobbing.

We went back to our seats and Dad stood up and kissed us both on the cheek. He was more composed than anyone during that ceremony. Then came the playing of Mario Lanza's 'Because', the song Mum and Dad played at their wedding. I remember it going for a long time—one of those songs where you think it has finished and then comes another verse.

The celebrant returned to the podium to farewell everyone who had turned out to farewell Mum. He then announced that as a fitting final tribute, we would be playing 'Que Sera, Sera', and encouraged everyone to stand, link arms and sing along. As I started to sing, I looked around at all the people in the room: every single one of them was singing. Singing and smiling. We had managed to turn this into a celebration after all. Mum would have loved it.

The song finished and everyone sat back down while the celebrant said a few final words. During this time, a huge beige velvet curtain began to move off to the right of the celebrant, making its way around the coffin, encircling it in a farewell tribute of its own. I realised that it probably wasn't going to clear my husband seated at the end of the row. Still, I was powerless to do anything about it. As the curtain came closer and closer, there was nowhere for him to go, so I leant over and whispered, 'I think you're going with her. Send me a message from the other side.'

He smiled and then, just like that, he was gone. Engulfed by a huge beige velvet curtain. What's the best way to reappear from behind a huge velvet curtain at a funeral? I probably would have barrel-rolled out and jumped up with my arms out, like I'd just landed a triple-pike inverted full-twisted somersault. He sensibly just walked to the end of the curtain and assimilated back into the crowd. I almost called out, 'Here he is, back from the dead!' but didn't.

We had requested that Mum's ashes be divided into four equal parts, so we'd each be able to treasure her. She had never talked about wanting her ashes sprinkled anywhere in particular—once again confirming that we weren't the kind of family that planned ahead.

Mum's sister, who had passed a few years before, had, as previously established, been a diehard Collingwood fan, and in 1990 my brother and I went to the AFL grand final with her. As the siren sounded to end the game, with Collingwood victorious, my aunt handed my brother a small container and asked him to climb the fence and tip the container onto the middle of the ground. When he enquired what was in the container, she replied, 'Your uncle.' My uncle, who had passed a year or two prior to that game, wasn't much of a football fan, but it was where *she* wanted his ashes scattered, and she had waited and hoped that the opportunity would finally present itself, which it finally did.

My husband's grandmother, who died at the age of 98, wanted her ashes scattered at Columbia Gorge, a spectacularly beautiful spot in Portland, Oregon. She was quite a character, and when I first met her she was well into her nineties and still living at home in Atlantic City. She was also a smoker, and whenever I tried to remind her about the health risks of smoking, she would always respond the same way: 'Don't you tell me not to smoke, I am 94 years old and I will smoke if I want to.' She had a point.

Shortly after she died, my husband and I drove to the gorge with his parents, to scatter her ashes. As we all stood together on the edge of a bridge overlooking the most breathtaking view, my father-in-law tipped her ashes out of the container—just as a gust of wind hit. Grandma's ashes took flight and flew back up into our faces. Now there's a nice slice of karma for you. I guess Grandma got the last word on the smoking argument.

So Mum went off to be cremated, and everyone came back to our house for a party. It was good as it kept my mind occupied with serving up food and drinks. Every room I walked into was full of laughter, with stories about Mum flying around. By the time my son came home from school the crowd had dwindled a little, but my two cousins (daughters of my mum's sister) were still in fine form, helped along with a few bubbles. My poor boy didn't know what hit him when he walked in the house. I hadn't told him we were having a funeral—but he knew that he was in a house full of people who loved his nana and he sat and listened to every last story. Including one from my uncle, who revealed that Mum's grandfather was a travelling performer who apparently toured the world with a performing rooster, in a show called George and His Performing Cock. I did think about Googling him for more information, but I'm pretty sure an internet search of 'George and his performing cock' would see me end up on some national watchlist.

Everyone finally left, and the house felt very empty that night. Even though Mum had never set foot in our current house, she had always been with us in spirit, and much of our existence for the past thirteen years had centred around her care—but that night, something was different. A chapter had closed on our family life. A long, painful and exhausting chapter. Mum was finally at peace, and free of that hideous disease that had robbed her of a full and happy elderly life with her husband, children and grandchildren. She would have loved our son, and he would have adored her. She was everything you would expect a nana to be: generous, funny, caring, loving and a bit crazy.

That night as I was kissing my son goodnight, he asked if I missed Nana. I told him I did, sensing we were about to have an emotional conversation about how Nana is no longer with us in person, but will always be with us in spirit. He got up from his bed and hugged me.

'It's okay, Mum,' he said, pulling away to look at my face. 'She's up in heaven with Michael Jackson and he is looking after her now.'

I excused myself and walked out to the kitchen to talk to my husband.

'Have you ever mentioned Michael Jackson to Sam?'

'Nope,' he replied, looking justifiably confused.

I walked back into my son's room, gave him another kiss, and told him that I thought Nana would probably prefer to have Frank Sinatra looking after her—but I'm sure Michael Jackson would do a fine job too.

25

Life goes on

We have a little shrine for Mum on the mantelshelf. It's the same photo in the painted gold frame that adorned her coffin. I keep a little vase of fresh flowers next to it, and on special days I'll light the candle that sits on the other side. Our share of Mum's ashes will also go on the mantel in a smallish urn, which I am yet to purchase as I am yet to find the perfect container for such an honour.

The box containing her actual ashes is sitting in the bookshelf in our office. I tried to open the box only once, but it is clearly made by the same people who manufacture the black boxes for aircraft. I couldn't get the seal off it, and when I called the crematorium for advice they told me that it was indeed hard to open, and if you do get the seal off and try to transfer the ashes into another container, then you should probably do it over newspaper, as some of the ashes will most likely fall out. What? That seemed a bit cavalier to me—they just tip the ashes into this black plastic box and seal it shut. How will I know whether I got all of Mum out of there, and then do I just throw that old container in the trash? There would be residual ashes left inside.

So, Mum's ashes are still sitting there, sealed in that black container.

Dad looks at that photo of Mum on the mantel every time he walks into our lounge room, and on the nights he stays over he walks up to it, kisses his fingers and places them on her forehead, saying, 'Goodnight, my beautiful.'

We loaded stacks of photos of Mum onto Dad's iPhone, and I often find him just sitting by the window swiping through them—smiling.

I was always worried how Dad would cope after Mum's death. You hear so many stories about how one partner dies and then other follows suit with a broken heart. But he was fit, and still a relatively spritely spring chicken at the age of 84. He lasted about a month living with us before he got itchy feet—either that or the constant noise that comes from sharing a house with a five-year-old did his head in. So he moved back into his own unit, and stays at our house a few nights a week.

His routine for the past six years was to spend all day sitting with Mum, so I was worried he would be bored and have nothing to do. I shouldn't have. He has managed to carve out a nice new little routine for himself. Every morning he goes to the nursing home for coffee and tends to the gardens. Then he does a bit of grocery shopping at the supermarket, goes home to potter around his garden, then cooks himself dinner and finishes the night off with a glass of red wine and a bit of André Rieu.

The nights he is not with us, I phone him to check how his day has been. It took a while for me to not just automatically ask how Mum is.

Instead he asks me how the book is coming along.

'Getting there,' I say.

I think I might just go and call him now, to tell him I have finished.

Now, if only I could remember where I've put my phone.

Helpful websites and organisations

Search the internet for Alzheimer's or dementia and you will get literally millions of results. In Australia, there are many organisations that offer support and information for not only those who have Alzheimer's or dementia but equally as important, for those who are caring for loved ones. I have listed some websites that you may find useful but this is really just the tip of the iceberg. Be resourceful and don't be afraid to ask for help.

The most useful organisation for us was Alzheimer's Australia, a good place to start. They have a very comprehensive website that covers every aspect of dealing with Alzheimer's and dementia including care and support, suggested medical professionals, fact sheets and the latest news and research information. Their helpsheets are updated as new information is learned and research developments come to light. You can sign up for their newsletters that will keep you up to date with the latest dementia news. They have resources listed that are specific to each state so you can get information that is locally relevant. Their website is <https://fightdementia.org.au>.

If you don't have access to a computer—or you are like my parents were and have a perfectly good computer in the home but have no clue as to how to, or desire to, use it—then there is a number you can call, the Australian National Dementia Helpline, which will point you in the right direction for any enquiry regarding Alzheimer's and dementia. The number is 1800 100 500.

Another helpful organisation is Dementia Care Australia. They are an independent information and education organisation that specialises in all things Alzheimer's and dementia. They also offer a very comprehensive website with all of the information and resources listed, but they also offer a service where family members and carers can sign up to become a 'Spark of Life Member'. This offers suggestions and solutions to everyday problems that come from caring for a loved one with Alzheimer's or dementia. Their website is <www.dementiacareaustralia.com>.

The Alzheimer's Association is a voluntary health organisation that focuses on Alzheimer's care, support and research. Their website is very comprehensive in providing education, resources and awareness of Alzheimer's. Go to <www.alz.org/au/dementia-alzheimers-australia.asp>.

'Your Brain Matters' is a program developed by Alzheimer's Australia designed to help you look after your brain health. Rather than just give you the stock standard stats, information and tips on how to improve your brain health, it offers them up on a cute little website platform that may even feel like fun when doing it. They offer five steps for you to follow that may help to keep your brain healthy, set challenges for you and offer a range of quizzes that you can take to get a sense of where you are at. This can all be accessed from their website at <http://yourbrainmatters.org.au> or, to take it a step further, from this website you can download the BrainyApp app for your computer or phone and have the luxury of testing your grey matter whenever and wherever you are: <http://brainyapp.com.au/aus/>.

If you are like me and feel the need to Google palliative care so you look like you actually know what it entails, then go to this website for more information: <http://palliativecare.org.au>.

If you feel that your loved one's driving skills are a little more worrying that just the unfairly stereotypical 'old person behind the wheel' scenario, you might want to check out <https://vic.fightdementia.org.au/vic/about-dementia-and-memory-loss/dementia-and-driving>.

If you want an actual legitimate source for the three and seven stages of Alzheimer's rather that the stages I have listed in the book, then go to: <www.helpguide.org/articles/alzheimers-dementia/alzheimers-disease.htm>.

As mentioned on page 32, to download any of the versions of the SAGE test go to <http://wexnermedical.osu.edu/patient-care/healthcare-services/brain-spine-neuro/memory-disorders/sage#SAGE%20Test>. If you are in Australia it is probably best to download the 'English (NZ)' version as these versions have fewer quarter, nickel and dime references.

Louis Theroux's documentary *Extreme Love: Dementia* is not available to watch online at the time this book was printed. If you want further information about the documentary you can find it at: <https://en.wikipedia.org/wiki/Extreme_Love:_Dementia>. There is also an IMDB site for it: <www.imdb.com/title/tt2371383/> and if you want your own personal copy then you can purchase it from the iTunes store: <https://itunes.apple.com/au/tv-season/louis-theroux-extreme-love/id520802107>.

Here is a link to the YouTube clip on Naomi Feil and use of validation therapy with Gladys Wilson. Try to watch that one without crying! <www.youtube.com/watch?v=CrZXz10FcVM>

Here are some other useful online resources that Alzheimer's Australia have suggested might be worth a look:

<www.fightdementia.org.au/national/about-us/campaigns/dementia-friendly-communities>
<www.dementialearning.org.au>
<www.isitdementia.com.au>
<www.dementiaresearchfoundation.org.au>
<www.detectearly.org.au>

\<www.helpwithdementia.org.au\>
\<www.isitdementia.com.au\>
\<www.livingwellwithdementia.org.au\>
\<www.start2talk.org.au\>
\<www.talkdementia.org.au\>
\<www.valuingpeople.org.au\>

Self-Administered Gerocognitive Exam

How Well Are You Thinking?

Please complete this form in ink **without** the assistance of others.

Name_____ Date of Birth _____/_____/_____

How far did you get in school? _____ I am a Man_____ Woman_____

I am NZ European_____ Māori _____ P acific Islander_____ Asian_____ Other_____

Have you had any problems with memory or thinking?   Yes_____ Only Occasionally_____ No_____

Have you had any blood relatives that have had problems with memory or thinking? Yes_____ No_____

Do you have balance problems?   Yes_____ No_____

       If yes, do you know the cause? Yes (specify reason)_____ No____

Have you ever had a major stroke? Yes_____ No_____A minor or mini-stroke? Yes_____ No_____

Do you currently feel sad or depressed?   Yes_____ Only Occasionally_____ No_____

Have you had any change in your personality? Yes (specify changes)_____ No_____

Do you have more difficulties doing everyday activities due to thinking problems? Yes_____No_____

---

1. **What is today's date?** (from memory – no cheating!) Month_____ Date_____ Year_____

---

2. **Name the following pictures** (don't worry about spelling):

_____   _____

CONTINUE NEXT PAGE ⟩

Answer these questions:

3. How are a rose and a tulip similar? Write down how they are alike. They both are… what?

_____

4. How many 20 cent pieces are in $5.40? _____

5. You are buying $3.10 of groceries. How much change would you receive back from a $5 note?

_____

6. Memory Test (memorize these instructions). Do later only after completing this entire test:

At the bottom of the very last page: Write "I have finished" on the blank line provided

7. Copy this picture:

8. Drawing test

- Draw a large face of a clock and place in the numbers
- Position the hands for 10 minutes before 11 o'clock
- On your clock, label "L" for the long hand and "S" for the short hand

CONTINUE NEXT PAGE >

9. Write down the names of 12 different <u>countries</u> located anywhere in the world (don't worry about spelling):

_____   _____   _____   _____

_____   _____   _____   _____

_____   _____   _____   _____

Review this example (this first one is done for you) then go to question 10 below: Draw a line from one circle to another starting at 1 and alternating numbers and letters (1 to A to 2 to B to 3 to C).

10. Do the following: Draw a line from one circle to another starting at 1 and alternating numbers and letters in order before ending at F (1 to A to 2 to B and so on).

D. Scharre MD, version 6.13 http://sagetest.osu.edu   **Page 3 of 5**

CONTINUE NEXT PAGE

Review this <u>example</u> (this first one is done for you) then answer question 11 below:
- Beginning with 6 squares
- Cross out 1 line (marked with an X)
- Leaving 5 squares
- Each line must be part of a complete square (no extra lines).

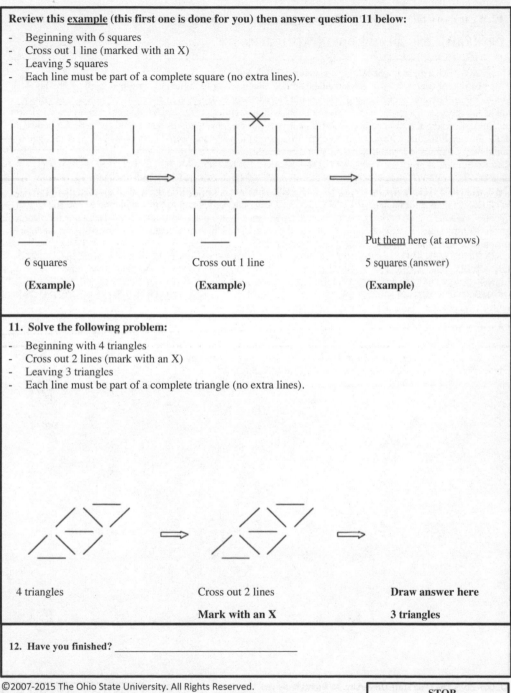

Put them here (at arrows)

6 squares	Cross out 1 line	5 squares (answer)
(Example)	**(Example)**	**(Example)**

11. **Solve the following problem:**
- Beginning with 4 triangles
- Cross out 2 lines (mark with an X)
- Leaving 3 triangles
- Each line must be part of a complete triangle (no extra lines).

4 triangles   Cross out 2 lines   **Draw answer here**

Mark with an X   3 triangles

12. **Have you finished?** _____

STOP

Explanation of SAGE Scoring

Please note that SAGE screening is not a diagnostic test of any condition. Our research has shown that SAGE can often, but not always, indicate whether individuals fall into the normal range, have mild memory or thinking impairments, or have a more severe memory or thinking condition. Please see the table below.

SAGE Score (Maximum Score=22)	Interpretation
17 to 22	Individuals with these scores are very likely to be *normal*.
15 and 16	Individuals with these scores are likely to have *mild memory or thinking impairments.* Further evaluation by a physician is recommended.
14 and below	Individuals with these scores are likely to have a *more severe memory or thinking condition.* Further evaluation by a physician is recommended.

Reference: Scharre DW, Chang S-I, Murden RA, Lamb J, Beversdorf DQ, Kataki M, Naharaja HN, Bornstein RA: Self-administered Gerocognitive Examination (SAGE): A brief cognitive assessment instrument for Mild Cognitive Impairment (MCI) and early dementia. Alzheimer Dis Assoc Disord 2010;24:64-71

Self-Administered Gerocognitive Examination (SAGE) Administration and Scoring Instructions

SAGE is a brief self-administered cognitive screening instrument to identify Mild Cognitive Impairment (MCI) and early dementia. Average time to complete the test is 15 minutes. The maximum score is 22. A score of 17 and above is considered normal.

Administration:

The test is self-administered. It should be filled out in ink without the assistance of others. Inform the examinee that there are four pages to complete. Calendars and clocks should not be available during the testing. Do not answer specific questions. Just say, "Do the best that you can".

Non-Scored Items:

Demographics

Insight: Have you had any problems with memory or thinking?

Family History

Motor symptoms Stroke

symptoms Depression

symptoms Personality

changes Functional abilities

Scored Items:

1. Orientation: Total possible points are 4

Month:	1	=	Correct
	0	=	Incorrect
Date:	2	=	exact
	1	=	± 3 days
	0	=	All else
Year:	1	=	Correct
	0	=	Incorrect

2. Naming: Total possible points are 2. Correct spelling not required.

Each Picture: 1   =   Correct
                  0   =   Incorrect

3. Similarities: Total possible points are 2. Correct spelling/grammar not required.
                  2   =   Abstract
                  1   =   Concrete
                  0   =   All else

4. Calculation: Total possible point is 1.
                  1   =   Correct
                  0   =   Incorrect

5. Calculation: Total possible point is 1.
                  1   =   Correct
                  0   =   Incorrect

6. Memory: Points given below in twelve.

7. Construction: Total possible points are 2.

3-D figure: 2   =   3-D, parallel lines within 10° and correct shape
                  1   =   3-D but lines not parallel within 10° or otherwise incorrect shape
                  0   =   All else

8. Construction: Total possible points are 2.

Clock: 4 components: Clock face, clock numbers (all 12 numbers in correct order clockwise and approximately correct quadrant position), hand positions (hands to correct time and must be joined near clock center), and hand size (actual or if labeled correctly)

                  2   =   4 of 4 components correct
                  1   =   3 of 4 components correct; one of the three correct components must be hand positions
                  0   =   All else

9. Verbal fluency: Total possible points are 2. Correct spelling not required.
                  2   =   12 different items listed
                  1   =   10 or 11 different items listed
                  0   =   9 or less different items listed

10. Executive: Modified Trails:	Total possible points are 2. An error is if two items that should be connected are not or if two items that should not be connected are.

2	=	Perfect or self-corrected errors only
1	=	1 or 2 errors
0	=	More than 2 errors

11. Executive: Total possible points are 2.
Problem solving: Forms 1 and 2:

2	=	Correct lines moved or marked **and** final diagram correct
1	=	Correct lines moved or marked **and** no final diagram drawn **Or** Correct lines moved or marked **but** final diagram incorrect **Or** No lines moved or marked **and** final diagram correct
0	=	All else including lines moved or marked incorrectly **but** final diagram correct

Forms 3 and 4:

2	=	Correct lines crossed out **and** final diagram correct
1	=	Correct lines crossed out **and** no final diagram drawn **Or** Correct lines crossed out **but** final diagram Incorrect **Or** No lines crossed out **and** final diagram correct
0	=	All else including lines crossed out incorrectly **but** final diagram correct

12. Memory: Total possible points are 2.
Forms 1 and 2:

2	=	Exact wording only, nothing extra: "I am done"
1	=	Must contain the word "done": "Yes, I am done", "done", others
0	=	All else

Forms 3 and 4:

2	=	Exact wording only, nothing extra: "I have finished"
1	=	Must contain the word "finished": "Yes, I have finished", "I am finished", "finished", others
0	=	All else

Total points = 0 (minimum) – 22 (maximum)

Acknowledgements

This was not an easy book to write. I had lived through watching my mother suffer with Alzheimer's for close to thirteen years and by the time I had finished writing it, she had been gone two years. I had to relive the story all over again, and it was a much more emotional journey than I could have imagined.

One doesn't just 'get through' something like this—one is nurtured and carried through, with love and support and encouragement, which I was lucky enough to have in spades.

So heartfelt thanks must be acknowledged to so many wonderful people.

Firstly to my wonderful husband, Ed, who took up a full-time job after being Mr Mum for seven years so I could put all my energy into writing while he put all his wages into our bank account. Your support was and is invaluable—and as a published author yourself, it must have been hard to sit back and watch without touching.

To my beautiful son, Sam. Your unconditional love and need for me to still be your mum outside the hours of 9 a.m. to 3 p.m. were what motivated me to keep writing. Every time I bring out a book for him to read, he asks me if it's my book. This time, buddy, it *is* my book, and you are reading it—finally! I love you more than I hate spiders.

To my sister, Jenni. We endured this thirteen-year journey together and you have always been the strong, sensible and rational one, keeping me grounded and talking me off the ledges that Dad occasionally puts me on.

To my brother, Peter. Sorry for painting you into a bullying big brother who never cries—it's called poetic licence. Thanks for being there and for being such a great support to Dad. And thanks to Peter's wife, Jules, for keeping Pete on track. Thanks to my nieces and nephews, Erinn, Jordan, Jordan and Lachlan. You guys rock and Nana adored you all.

To my American family, Mom, Dad, Julia, Rob, Vicky, Ken, Cathy and Rob and all of your wonderful kiddos—thanks for all the support and encouragement.

To my beautiful cousins, Gail Johnson and Debbie Pratt, and their amazing families. Mum loved you both like daughters. Thanks for sharing stories of your own mum for the book—she was a cracker!

Thanks to the many family friends who over the course of our family's life have been consistent and caring in their love and support. The Orrs, the Febens, the Storays and the Bennells.

To my gorgeous friends Stephanie Bansemer-Brown, Simone Desmond-McRostie and Andrea Stevens. You all kept me motivated with encouragement and love and the occasional much needed distraction. And for all of those friends who checked in on me and supported my journey—Rove, Johnny T, Hayley, Lozza, Lisa, Melissa, Mrs. C, Fary and all of my 'school mums'.

To Kaz Cooke, who kickstarted me and guided me down the right path—thanks for your advice and encouragement.

And to Declan Fay, who taught me more about writing than I ever needed to know. I guess all those hours I spent watching you lean back in your chair rubbing your belly have finally paid off. All good, not sad.

To all of the wonderful carers at Mum's nursing home who looked after her like she was family, and in turn looked after Dad along the way. Thanks to Linda and Pina for being there for Dad and keeping him caffeinated. To all the amazing people who have watched and cared for friends and loved ones with this disease. Thank you for sharing your stories with me. I am forever in debt for the inspiration and stimulation you gave me to write a book like this.

Lastly and mostly, Mum and Dad.

Mum, you always were and always will be the most loving, generous, supportive and beautiful person I have ever known. I hope you are proud of this book, and that I haven't embarrassed you too much by sharing our crazy family stories. I know you and Aunt Des are up there having a cuppa and spelling out swear words. I miss you and love you forever.

And Dad—words cannot convey how much you mean to me. You have been such an incredible role model for not just me, but everyone lucky enough to call you a friend or relative. Your unwavering love for Mum and our family is awe-inspiring. Thanks for supporting my quest in writing this book and giving me free rein to tell our story. I would tell you I love you more often, but without your hearing aids in you probably won't hear me. Lucky you already know.

SATIAMIME Test (Self-Administered, Totally Inconclusive and Mildly Irrelevant Memory Exam)

Here is my own version of a cognitive written test. I'm pretty sure it has little actual value in terms of keeping your brain active, and any score you get has no medical bearing whatsoever.

1 What present had my brother always received on Christmas Day?
   a) A bag of coal
   b) Chocolate-filled Santa stocking
   c) A pair of black lace G-strings

2 What item of my mother's did my father hang from a chandelier one morning?
   a) Her false teeth
   b) Her bra
   c) Her tiara

3 What favourite childhood toy did I sell for $5 at the garage sale?
   a) Barbie campervan
   b) BB gun
   c) A voodoo doll of my brother

4 What did I frame and give to my parents as a gift for their first Christmas in their new retirement village?
   a) A photo of André Rieu
   b) Our baby's twelve-week ultrasound
   c) A photo of their three children with only the top of my head in frame

5 How many Australians are currently diagnosed with dementia?
   a) Around 350,000
   b) 10,000,000
   c) What was the question again?

6 What was my auntie hoarding in the back of her drawers?
   a) André Rieu DVDs
   b) Other residents' reading glasses
   c) A six-pack of beer

7 What collective noun did I coin to describe a group of
Alzheimer's patients?
a) A wander
b) A forget
c) A muddle

8 Which DVD was on high rotation at my parents' house?
a) André Rieu
b) *The Muppets Take Manhattan*
c) *The Benny Hill Show*

9 What was my mother's all-time favourite song?
a) 'Gangnam Style'
b) 'Somewhere Over the Rainbow'
c) 'Baby Got Back'

10 In my grandmother-in-law's nursing home, what nickname
was on the door of another woman's room?
a) Grandma Funk
b) Grandma Hugs
c) Grandma InDaHouse

11 What type of man in uniform would turn up to my
mother's nursing home when Dot raised the alarm?
a) A fireman
b) A Chippendale
c) A janitor

12 What type of animal reading the news did I think would be a ratings bonanza?
   a) A monkey
   b) A comedian
   c) A dog

13 What type of biscuit did I obsess over in the bereavement holding pen?
   a) A Tim Tam
   b) An orange cream
   c) A hash cookie

14 What was Sam going to miss most about his nana?
   a) Her warm hugs
   b) Her baking
   c) Her wheelchair

15 Who did Sam reassuringly let me know was looking after Nana in heaven?
   a) Jesus
   b) Frank Sinatra
   c) Michael Jackson

Answers

Q1: b; Q2: a; Q3: a; Q4: b; Q5: a; Q6: b; Q7: a; Q8: a; Q9: b; Q10: b; Q11: a; Q12: c; Q13: b; Q14: c; Q15: c.

Calculating your score

Each correct answer is worth 3 points.
Each incorrect answer is worth 0 points.
Maximum points: 45
Minimum points: 0

Interpreting your score

30–45 points

Congratulations, you either have a very good memory, paid close attention to what you were reading, or you are a relative or friend of mine and knew the answers anyway. Either way you have nothing to worry about and can freely use 'it must be the Alzheimer's' comments willy-nilly in any social situation. Perhaps pick up the book in a year's time and do the test again and see how smart you feel then. If you can't remember where you have put the book, then go to the results summary of 0–14 points and have a read—it will probably apply to you then.

15–29 points

Not a bad result. You either read this book while riding the train to work, read it while in bed and dozed off during the last couple of pages each night, only found it mildly compelling and just skimmed it to see if anything might apply to you or a loved one, or your memory is not what it used to be and, judging from most of the made-up answers, your commonsense is possibly not up to scratch either. If none of the above apply to you and you just can't remember much of what you have just read, then maybe a trip to the doc is not a bad idea.

0–14 points

Well, at least you can hide your own Christmas presents this year.